Volume 2

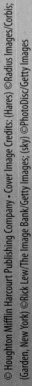

Made in the United States
Text printed on 100%
recycled paper

Houghton
Mifflin
Harcourt

ISBN 978-0-544-43270-3

10 0868 22 21 20 19 18 17

4500661134   D E F G

Dear Students and Families,

Welcome to **Go Math!**, Kindergarten! In this exciting mathematics program, there are hands-on activities to do and real-world problems to solve. Best of all, you will write your ideas and answers right in your book. In **Go Math!**, writing and drawing on the pages helps you think deeply about what you are learning, and you will really understand math!

By the way, all of the pages in your **Go Math!** book are made using recycled paper. We wanted you to know that you can Go Green with **Go Math!**

Sincerely,

The Authors

Made in the United States
Text printed on 100% recycled paper

GO MATH!

Authors

Juli K. Dixon, Ph.D.
Professor, Mathematics Education
University of Central Florida
Orlando, Florida

Edward B. Burger, Ph.D.
President, Southwestern University
Georgetown, Texas

Steven J. Leinwand
Principal Research Analyst
American Institutes for
    Research (AIR)
Washington, D.C.

Contributor

Rena Petrello
Professor, Mathematics
Moorpark College
Moorpark, CA

Matthew R. Larson, Ph.D.
K-12 Curriculum Specialist for
    Mathematics
Lincoln Public Schools
Lincoln, Nebraska

Martha E. Sandoval-Martinez
Math Instructor
El Camino College
Torrance, California

English Language Learners Consultant

Elizabeth Jiménez
CEO, GEMAS Consulting
Professional Expert on English
    Learner Education
Bilingual Education and
    Dual Language
Pomona, California

VOLUME 1
Number and Operations

 Critical Area Representing, relating, and operating on whole numbers, initially with sets of objects

1 Represent, Count, and Write Numbers 0 to 5 — **9**

Domains Counting and Cardinality
Operations and Algebraic Thinking

COMMON CORE STATE STANDARDS
K.CC.A.3, K.CC.B.4a, K.CC.B.4b, K.CC.B.4c, K.OA.A.3

2 Compare Numbers to 5 — **77**

Domain Counting and Cardinality

COMMON CORE STATE STANDARDS
K.CC.C.6

Critical Area

GO DIGITAL

Go online! Your math lessons are interactive. Use *iTools*, Animated Math Models, the Multimedia *eGlossary*, and more.

Chapter 1 Overview

In this chapter, you will explore and discover answers to the following **Essential Questions**:

- How can you show, count, and write numbers?
- How can you show numbers 0 to 5?
- How can you count numbers 0 to 5?
- How can you write numbers 0 to 5?

Chapter 2 Overview

In this chapter, you will explore and discover answers to the following **Essential Questions**:

- How can building and comparing sets help you compare numbers?
- How does matching help you compare sets?
- How does counting help you compare sets?
- How do you know if the number of counters in one set is the same as, greater than, or less than the number of counters in another set?

Chapter 3 Overview

In this chapter, you will explore and discover answers to the following **Essential Questions**:

- How can you show, count, and write numbers 6 to 9?
- How can you show numbers 6 to 9?
- How can you count numbers 6 to 9?
- How can you write numbers 6 to 9?

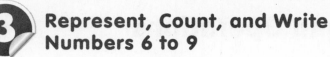

3 Represent, Count, and Write Numbers 6 to 9   115

Domain Counting and Cardinality
COMMON CORE STATE STANDARDS
K.CC.A.3, K.CC.B.5, K.CC.C.6, K.CC.C.7

Practice and Homework

Lesson Check and Spiral Review in every lesson

4 Represent and Compare Numbers to 10 — 177

Domains Counting and Cardinality
Operations and Algebraic Thinking
COMMON CORE STATE STANDARDS
K.CC.A.2, K.CC.A.3, K.CC.B.5, K.CC.C.6, K.CC.C.7, K.OA.A.3, K.OA.A.4

Chapter 4 Overview

In this chapter, you will explore and discover answers to the following **Essential Questions**:

- How can you show and compare numbers to 10?
- How can you count forward to 10?
- How can you show numbers from 1 to 10?
- How can using models help you compare two numbers?

5 Addition — 227

Domain Operations and Algebraic Thinking
COMMON CORE STATE STANDARDS
K.OA.A.1, K.OA.A.2, K.OA.A.3, K.OA.A.4, K.OA.A.5

Chapter 5 Overview

In this chapter, you will explore and discover answers to the following **Essential Questions**:

- How can you show addition?
- How can using objects or pictures help you show addition?
- How can you use numbers and symbols to show addition?

Personal Math Trainer
Online Assessment and Intervention

Personal Math Trainer
Online Assessment and Intervention

Domain Operations and Algebraic Thinking
COMMON CORE STATE STANDARDS
K.OA.A.1, K.OA.A.2, K.OA.A.5

Sheep and Ducks

7 · Represent, Count, and Write 11 to 19 · 357

Domains Counting and Cardinality
Number and Operations in Base Ten
COMMON CORE STATE STANDARDS
K.CC.A.3, K.NBT.A.1

Chapter 7 Overview

In this chapter, you will explore and discover answers to the following **Essential Questions**:

- How can you show, count, and write numbers 11 to 19?
- How can you show numbers 11 to 19?
- How can you read and write numbers 11 to 19?
- How can you show the teen numbers as 10 and some more?

8 · Represent, Count, and Write 20 and Beyond · 425

Domain Counting and Cardinality
COMMON CORE STATE STANDARDS
K.CC.A.1, K.CC.A.2, K.CC.A.3, K.CC.B.5, K.CC.C.6, K.CC.C.7

Chapter 8 Overview

In this chapter, you will explore and discover answers to the following **Essential Questions**:

- How can you show, count, and write numbers to 20 and beyond?
- How can you show and write numbers to 20?
- How can you count numbers to 50 by ones?
- How can you count numbers to 100 by tens?

GO DIGITAL

Go online! Your math lessons are interactive. Use *iTools*, Animated Math Models, the Multimedia *eGlossary*, and more.

Chapter 9 Overview

In this chapter, you will explore and discover answers to the following **Essential Questions**:

• How can you identify, name, and describe two-dimensional shapes?

• How can knowing the parts of two-dimensional shapes help you join shapes?

• How can knowing the number of sides and vertices of two-dimensional shapes help you identify shapes?

Personal Math Trainer
Online Assessment and Intervention

VOLUME 2
Geometry and Positions

Common Core **Critical Area** Describing shapes and space

Domain Geometry
COMMON CORE STATE STANDARDS
K.G.A.2, K.G.B.4, K.G.B.6

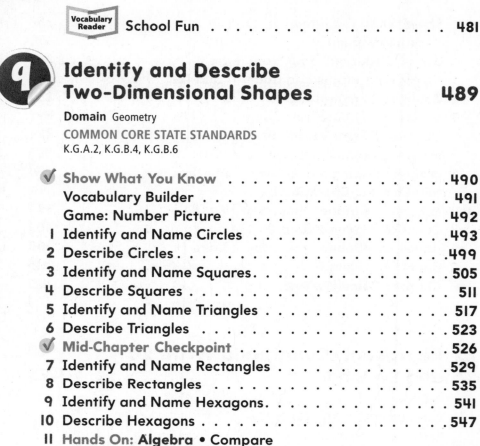

10 Identify and Describe Three-Dimensional Shapes   569

Domain Geometry

COMMON CORE STATE STANDARDS
K.G.A.1, K.G.A.2, K.G.A.3, K.G.B.4, K.G.B.5

Chapter 10 Overview

In this chapter, you will explore and discover answers to the following **Essential Questions**:

• How can identifying and describing shapes help you sort them?
• How can you describe three-dimensional shapes?
• How can you sort three-dimensional shapes?

Practice and Homework

Lesson Check and Spiral Review in every lesson

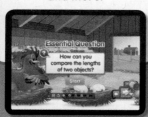

GO DIGITAL

Go online! Your math lessons are interactive. Use *i*Tools, Animated Math Models, the Multimedia *e*Glossary, and more.

Chapter 11 Overview

In this chapter, you will explore and discover answers to the following **Essential Questions**:

• How can comparing objects help you measure them?

• How can you compare the length of objects?

• How can you compare the height of objects?

• How can you compare the weight of objects?

Chapter 12 Overview

In this chapter, you will explore and discover answers to the following **Essential Questions**:

• How does sorting help you display information?

• How can you sort and classify objects by color?

• How can you sort and classify objects by shape?

• How can you sort and classify objects by size?

• How do you display information on a graph?

Measurement and Data

Common Core **Critical Area** Representing, relating, and operating on whole numbers, initially with sets of objects

 ## Measurement   **645**

Domain Measurement and Data
COMMON CORE STATE STANDARDS
K.MD.A.1, K.MD.A.2

Classify and Sort Data   **683**

Domain Measurement and Data
COMMON CORE STATE STANDARDS
K.MD.B.3

School Fun

written by Ann Dickson

Common Core **CRITICAL AREA** Describing shapes and space

1. Sign in.

2. Put your book bag away.

3. Choose a center.

Here is my classroom. Come on in.

Learning time is about to begin.

Social Studies

Why do we have rules?

These are the book bags

we hang by our names.

Circle the ones that look the same.

Social Studies

Why do we need to take turns?

Here are the books. We read them all!

Which books are big?

Which books are small?

Social Studies

Why do we help others?

Here are markers of every kind.

Name all of the colors that you can find.

Social Studies

Why do we put things away?

Our blocks and toys are over there.

Which shapes are round?

Which shapes are square?

Social Studies

Why do we share?

Write About the Story

DIRECTIONS These lunch boxes are alike. In one lunch box draw something that you like to eat. Now circle the lunch box that is different.

Alike and Different

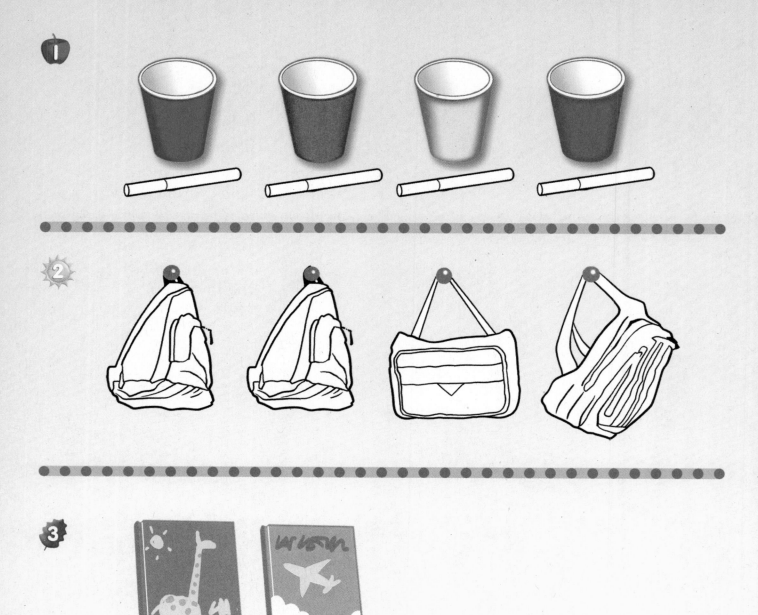

DIRECTIONS 1. Color the markers so that they match the colors of the cups.
2. Color the book bags that are alike by shape.   **3.** This classroom needs some books. Draw a book that is a different size.

Identify and Describe Two-Dimensional Shapes

Curious About Math with
Curious George

The sails on these boats are shaped like a triangle.

- How many stripes can you count on the first sail?

Name _____

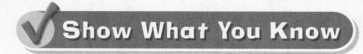Show What You Know

Personal Math Trainer
Online Assessment
and Intervention

Shape

 1

 2

 3

Count Objects

 4

_____

- - - - - - - -

_____

5

_____

- - - - - - - -

_____

6

_____

- - - - - - - -

_____

This page checks understanding of important skills needed for success in Chapter 9.

DIRECTIONS 1–3. Look at the shape at the beginning of the row.
Mark an X on the shape that is alike. 4–6. Count and tell how many.
Write the number.

© Houghton Mifflin Harcourt Publishing Company

490 four hundred ninety

Vocabulary Builder

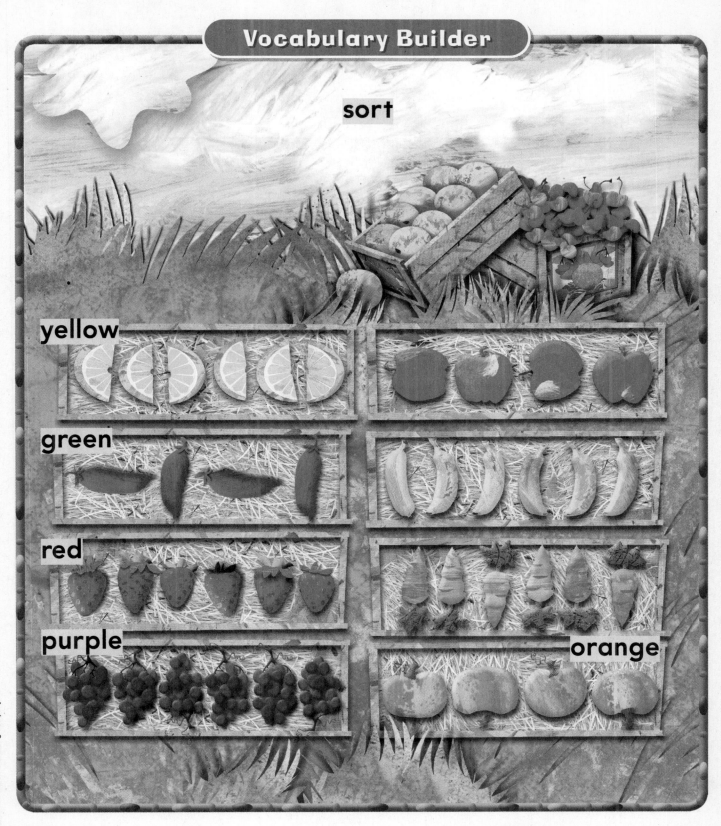

sort

yellow

green

red

purple

orange

DIRECTIONS Circle the box that is sorted by green vegetables. Mark an X on the box that is sorted by purple fruit.

GO DIGITAL
• **Interactive Student Edition**
• **Multimedia *eGlossary***

Game

Number Picture

DIRECTIONS Play with a partner. Decide who goes first.
Toss the number cube. Color a shape in the picture that matches
the number rolled. A player misses a turn if a number is rolled and
all shapes with that number are colored. Continue until all shapes
in the picture are colored.

MATERIALS number cube
(labeled 1, 2, 2, 3, 3, 4), crayons

Chapter 9 Vocabulary

alike

igual

3

circle

círculo

11

curve

curva

16

different

diferente

19

hexagon

hexágono

34

rectangle

rectángulo

52

side

lado

63

square

cuadrado

70

circle

alike

  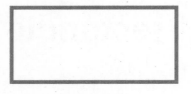

different

curve

rectangle

hexagon

square

side

Chapter 9 Vocabulary *(continued)*

triangle triángulo 79	**vertex** vértice 83
vertices vértices 84	**zero** cero, ninguno 86

vertex

triangle

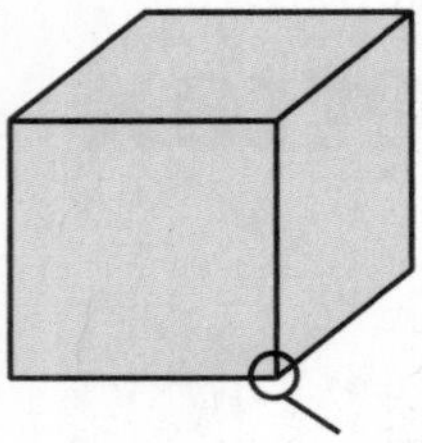

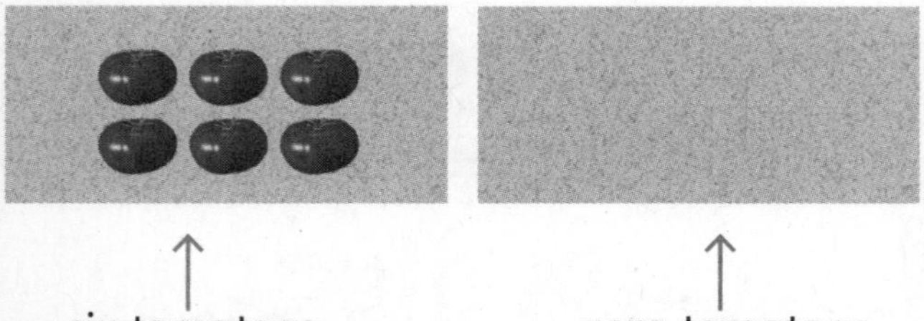

six tomatoes   zero tomatoes

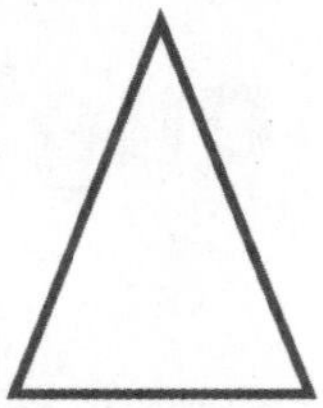

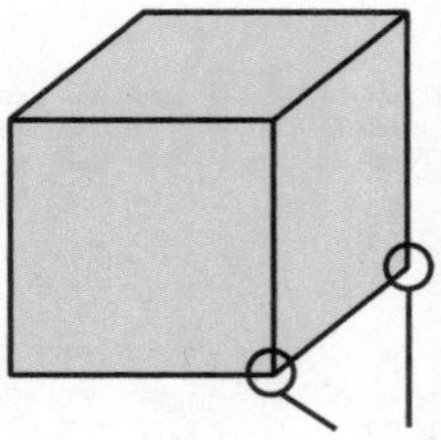

vertices

Shapes

circle

curve

hexagon

rectangle

side

square

triangle

vertex

DIRECTIONS Say each word. Tell something you know about the word.

Game

START

DIRECTIONS Place game pieces on START. Play with a partner. Take turns. Toss the number cube. Move that many spaces. If a player can name the shape and tell something about the shape, the player moves ahead 1 space. The first player to reach FINISH wins.

MATERIALS I connecting cube game piece for each player, number cube

© Houghton Mifflin Harcourt Publishing Company

492B four hundred ninety-two

The Write Way

DIRECTIONS Choose two shapes. Draw to show what you know about the shapes.
Reflect Be ready to tell about your drawing.

Name _____

Identify and Name Circles

Essential Question How can you identify and name circles?

Common Core Geometry—K.G.A.2

MATHEMATICAL PRACTICES
MP5, MP6, MP7

Listen and Draw

circles	not circles

DIRECTIONS Place two-dimensional shapes on the page. Identify and name the circles. Sort the shapes by circles and not circles. Trace and color the shapes on the sorting mat.

Chapter 9 • Lesson I

DIRECTIONS 1. Mark an X on all of the circles.

DIRECTIONS 2. Color the circles in the picture.

Problem Solving • Applications Real World

WRITE Math

3

4

DIRECTIONS 3. Neville puts his shapes in a row. Which shape is a circle? Mark an X on that shape. **4.** Draw to show what you know about circles. Tell a friend about your drawing.

HOME ACTIVITY • Have your child show you an object that is shaped like a circle.

Name _____

Identify and Name Circles

Common Core

COMMON CORE STANDARD—K.G.A.2
Identify and describe shapes (squares, circles, triangles, rectangles, hexagons, cubes, cones, cylinders, and spheres).

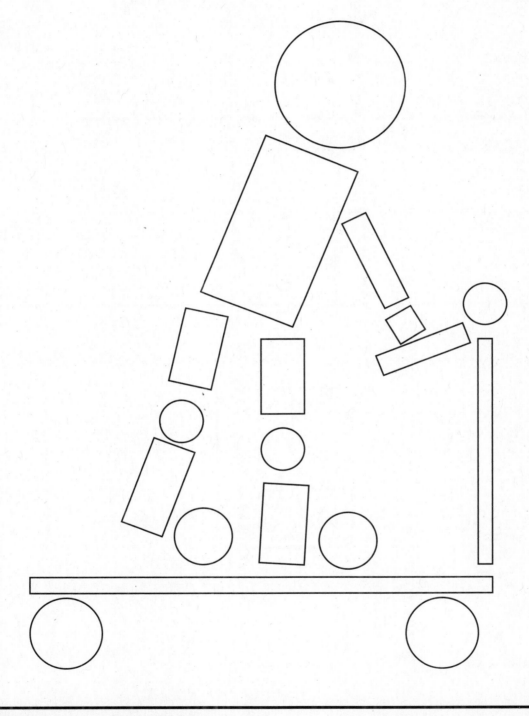

DIRECTIONS **1.** Color the circles in the picture.

Lesson Check (K.G.A.2)

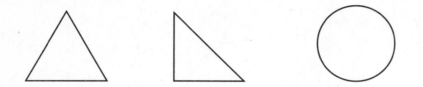

Spiral Review (K.CC.A.2, K.OA.A.2)

 2

1 5   1 7

 3

5 + _____ ═══ _____

DIRECTIONS **I.** Color the circle. **2.** Count forward. Trace and write the numbers in order. **3.** Trace and write to complete the addition sentence about the sets of cats.

FOR MORE PRACTICE GO TO THE Personal Math Trainer

Name _____

Describe Circles

Essential Question How can you describe circles?

Common Core Geometry—K.G.B.4

MATHEMATICAL PRACTICES
MP5, MP7

Listen and Draw *Real World*

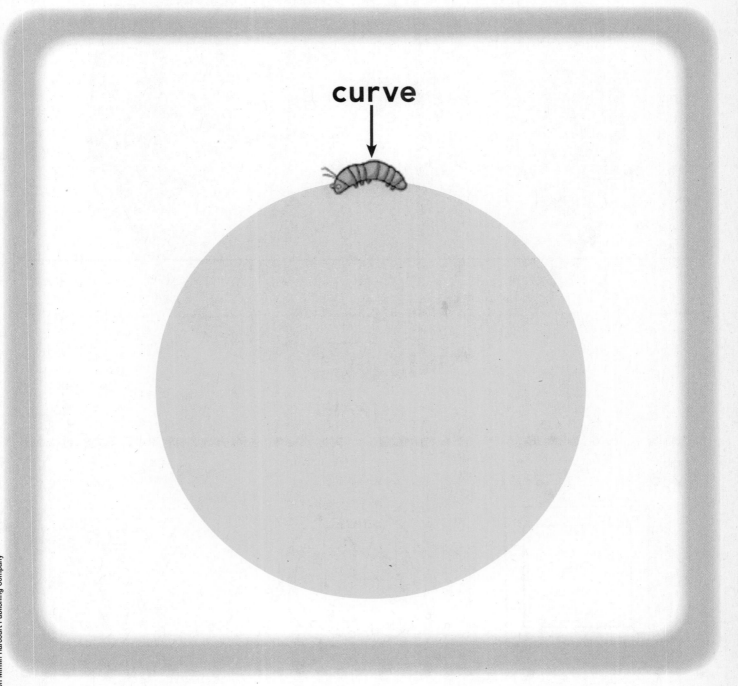

DIRECTIONS Use your finger to trace around the circle. Talk about the curve. Trace around the curve.

Chapter 9 • Lesson 2

1

circle

2 ✓

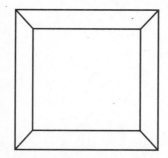

YIELD

DIRECTIONS **1.** Use your finger to trace around the circle. Trace the curve around the circle. **2.** Color the object that is shaped like a circle.

DIRECTIONS **3.** Use a pencil to hold one end of a large paper clip on one of the dots in the center of the page. Place another pencil in the other end of the paper clip. Move the pencil around to draw a circle.

Problem Solving • Applications

 4

DIRECTIONS 4. I have a curve. What shape am I? Draw the shape. Tell a friend the name of the shape.

 HOME ACTIVITY • Have your child describe a circle.

Describe Circles

 COMMON CORE STANDARD—K.G.B.4
Analyze, compare, create, and compose shapes.

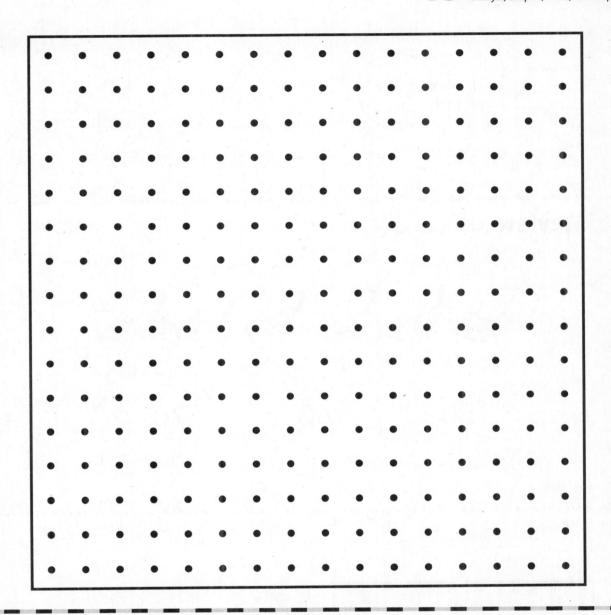

DIRECTIONS **1.** Use a pencil to hold one end of a large paper clip on one of the dots in the center. Place another pencil in the other end of the paper clip. Move the pencil around to draw a circle. **2.** Color the object that is shaped like a circle.

50   60   70

_____

- - - - - - - -

_____

DIRECTIONS **1.** Which shape has a curve? Color that shape.   **2.** Point to each set of 10 as you count by tens. Circle the number that shows how many grapes there are.   **3.** How many tiles are there? Write the number.

FOR MORE PRACTICE
GO TO THE
Personal Math Trainer

Name _____

Identify and Name Squares

Essential Question How can you identify and name squares?

Common Core Geometry—K.G.A.2

MATHEMATICAL PRACTICES
MP5, MP6, MP7

Listen and Draw Real World Hands On

squares	not squares

DIRECTIONS Place two-dimensional shapes on the page. Identify and name the squares. Sort the shapes by squares and not squares. Trace and color the shapes on the sorting mat.

Chapter 9 • Lesson 3

DIRECTIONS 1. Mark an X on all of the squares.

Name _____

DIRECTIONS 2. Color the squares in the picture.

Chapter 9 • Lesson 3

Problem Solving • Applications

3

4

DIRECTIONS **3.** Dennis drew these shapes. Which shapes are squares? Mark an X on those shapes. **4.** Draw to show what you know about squares. Tell a friend about your drawing.

HOME ACTIVITY • Have your child show you an object that is shaped like a square.

Identify and Name Squares

Common
Core

COMMON CORE STANDARD—K.G.A.2
Identify and describe shapes (squares, circles, triangles, rectangles, hexagons, cubes, cones, cylinders, and spheres).

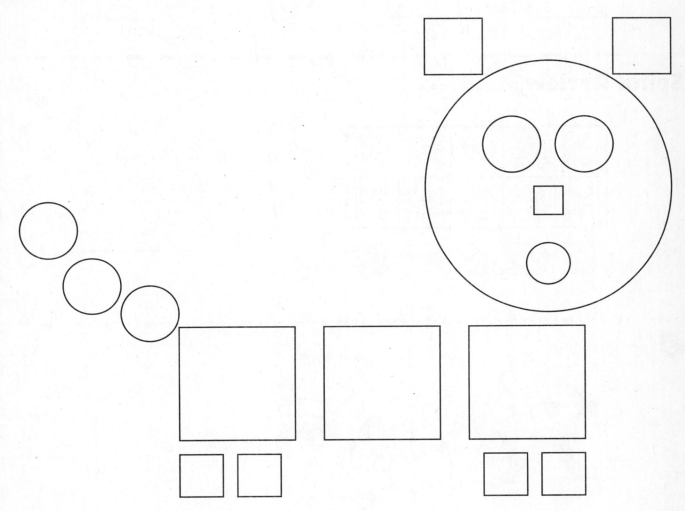

DIRECTIONS **1.** Color the squares in the picture.

Chapter 9

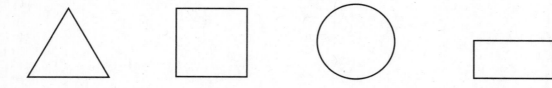

Spiral Review (K.CC.A.3, K.OA.A.1)

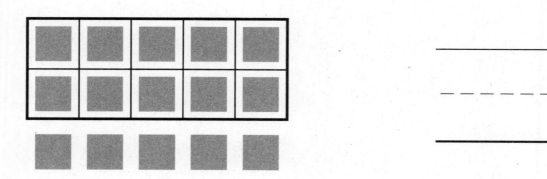

 and

DIRECTIONS 1. Which shape is a square? Color the square. 2. How many tiles are there? Write the number. 3. Trace the number of puppies. Trace the number of puppies being added. Write the number that shows how many puppies there are now.

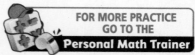

FOR MORE PRACTICE
GO TO THE
Personal Math Trainer

Name _____

Describe Squares

Essential Question How can you describe squares?

Common Core Geometry—K.G.B.4

MATHEMATICAL PRACTICES
MP2, MP7, MP8

Listen and Draw

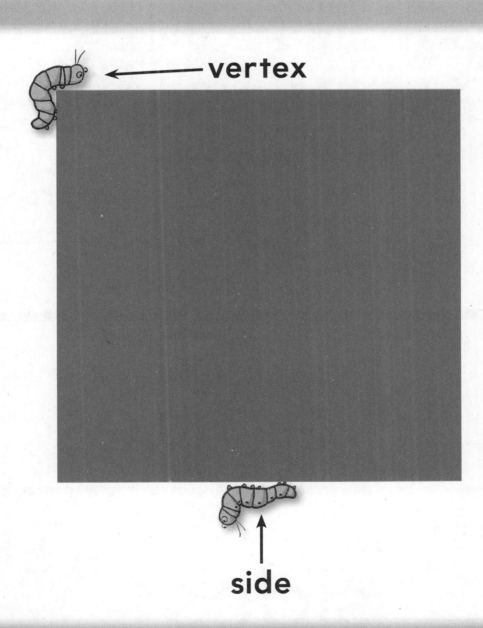

vertex

side

DIRECTIONS Use your finger to trace around the square. Talk about the number of sides and the number of vertices. Draw an arrow pointing to another vertex. Trace around the sides.

square

 ____

vertices

 ____

sides

DIRECTIONS 1. Place a counter on each corner, or vertex. Write how many corners, or vertices. 2. Trace around the sides. Write how many sides.

DIRECTIONS 3. Draw and color a square.

Chapter 9 • Lesson 4

Problem Solving • Applications

4

DIRECTIONS 4. I have 4 sides of equal length and 4 vertices. What shape am I? Draw the shape. Tell a friend the name of the shape.

HOME ACTIVITY • Have your child describe a square.

514 five hundred fourteen

Describe Squares

Common Core
COMMON CORE STANDARD—K.G.B.4
Analyze, compare, create, and compose shapes.

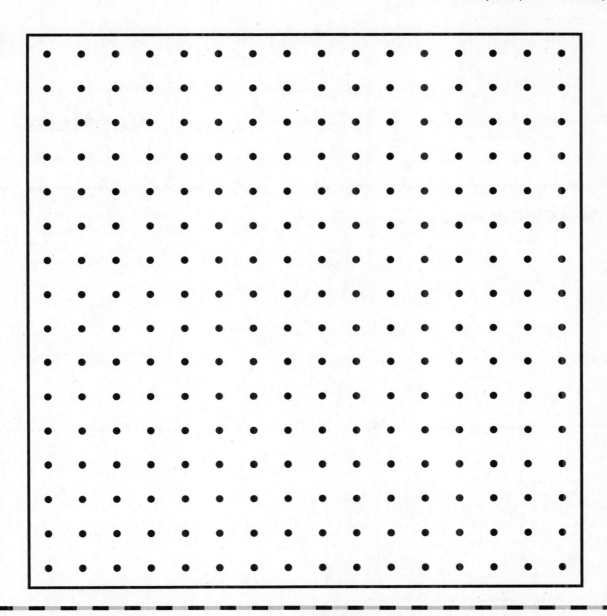

② _____ _____

_____ **vertices**

③ _____ _____

_____ **sides**

DIRECTIONS 1. Draw and color a square. 2. Place a counter on each corner, or vertex, of the square that you drew. Write how many corners, or vertices. 3. Trace around the sides of the square that you drew. Write how many sides.

Lesson Check (K.G.B.4)

_____

_ _ _ _ _ _

_____ **vertices**

Spiral Review (K.CC.A.3)

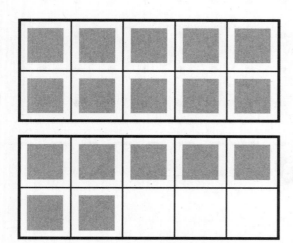

_____

_ _ _ _ _ _

_____

_____

_ _ _ _ _ _

_____

DIRECTIONS 1. How many vertices does the square have? Write the number. 2. Count and tell how many pieces of fruit. Write the number. 3. How many tiles are there? Write the number.

FOR MORE PRACTICE GO TO THE Personal Math Trainer

Identify and Name Triangles

Essential Question How can you identify and name triangles?

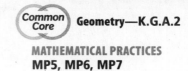 Geometry—K.G.A.2

MATHEMATICAL PRACTICES
MP5, MP6, MP7

Listen and Draw

triangles	not triangles

DIRECTIONS Place two-dimensional shapes on the page. Identify and name the triangles. Sort the shapes by triangles and not triangles. Trace and color the shapes on the sorting mat.

Name _____

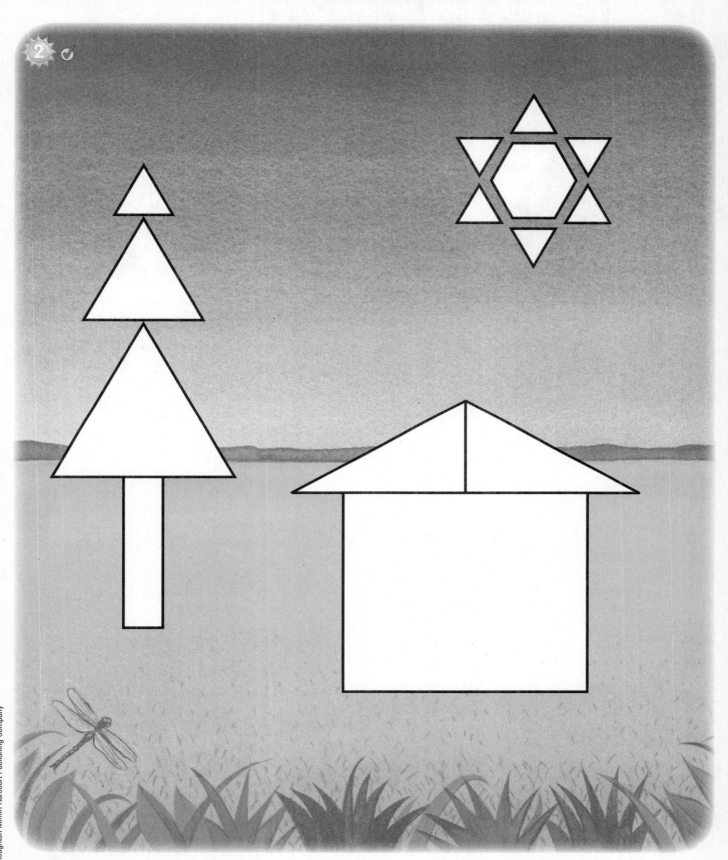

DIRECTIONS 2. Color the triangles in the picture.

Problem Solving • Applications Real World

WRITE Math

3

4

DIRECTIONS 3. Anita put her shapes in a row. Which shapes are triangles? Mark an X on those shapes. **4.** Draw to show what you know about triangles. Tell a friend about your drawing.

HOME ACTIVITY • Have your child show you an object that is shaped like a triangle.

Identify and Name Triangles

Common Core

COMMON CORE STANDARD—K.G.A.2
Identify and describe shapes (squares, circles, triangles, rectangles, hexagons, cubes, cones, cylinders, and spheres).

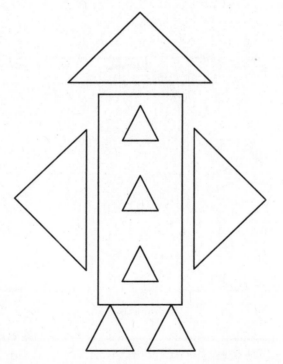

Lesson Check (K.G.A.2)

Spiral Review (K.CC.A.1, K.CC.B.5)

1	2	3	4	5	6	7	8	9	10
11	12	13	14	15	16	17	18	19	20
21	22	23	24	25	26	27	28	29	30

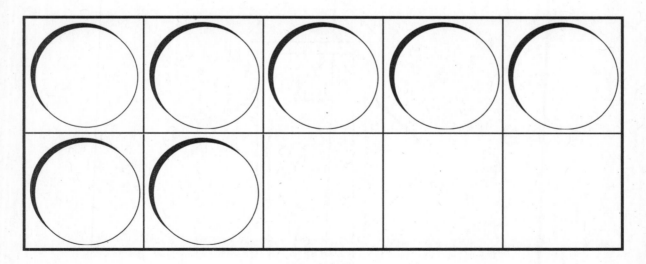

DIRECTIONS **1.** Which shape is a triangle? Color the triangle. **2.** Begin with 1 and count forward to 24. What is the next number? Draw a line under that number. **3.** How many more counters would you place to model a way to make 10? Draw the counters.

© Houghton Mifflin Harcourt Publishing Company

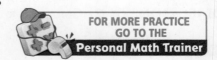

FOR MORE PRACTICE
GO TO THE
Personal Math Trainer

Name _____

Describe Triangles

Essential Question How can you describe triangles?

Common Core · Geometry—K.G.B.4

MATHEMATICAL PRACTICES
MP2, MP7, MP8

Listen and Draw

vertex

side

DIRECTIONS Use your finger to trace around the triangle. Talk about the number of sides and the number of vertices. Draw an arrow pointing to another vertex. Trace around the sides.

Chapter 9 • Lesson 6

triangle

 ☑ _____ **vertices**

 ☑ _____ **sides**

DIRECTIONS 1. Place a counter on each corner, or vertex. Write how many corners, or vertices. 2. Trace around the sides. Write how many sides.

Name _____

DIRECTIONS 3. Draw and color a triangle.

HOME ACTIVITY • Have your child describe a triangle.

Concepts and Skills

_____

_ _ _ _ _ sides

_____

_ _ _ _ _ vertices

_____

_ _ _ _ _ sides

_____

_ _ _ _ _ vertices

3 THINK SMARTER

   •

•      •

•

circle   square   triangle

DIRECTIONS 1–2. Trace around each side. Write how many sides. Place a counter on each corner or vertex. Write how many vertices. (K.G.B.4) **3.** Draw lines to match the shape to its name. (K.G.A.2)

Describe Triangles

 COMMON CORE STANDARD—K.G.B.4
Analyze, compare, create, and compose shapes.

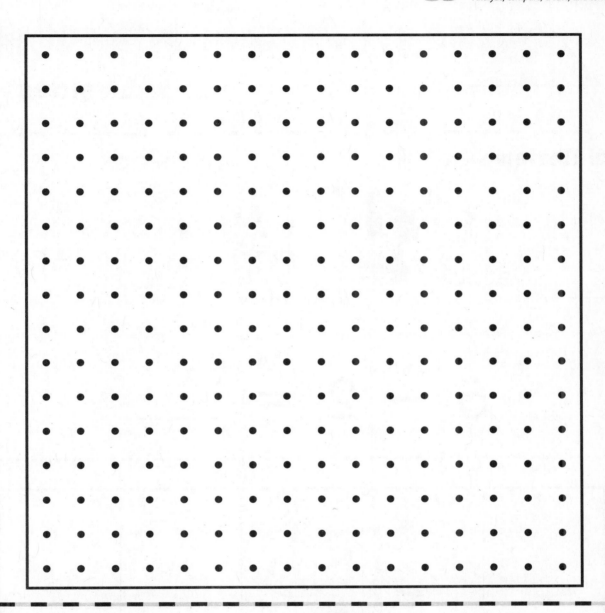

 _____ **vertices**

 _____ **sides**

DIRECTIONS **1.** Draw and color a triangle. **2.** Place a counter on each corner, or vertex, of the triangle that you drew. Write how many corners, or vertices. **3.** Trace around the sides of the triangle that you drew. Write how many sides.

Chapter 9

Lesson Check <small>(K.G.B.4)</small>

 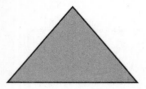

_____

- - - - - - -

_____ **sides**

Spiral Review <small>(K.CC.B.5, K.OA.A.1)</small>

5 – 2 = ____

_____

- - - - - - -

_____

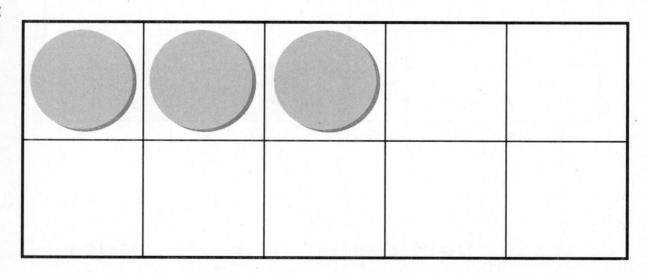

DIRECTIONS **1.** How many sides does the triangle have? Write the number. **2.** How many kittens are left? Write the number. **3.** How many more counters would you place to model a way to make 7? Draw the counters.

528 five hundred twenty-eight

 FOR MORE PRACTICE GO TO THE **Personal Math Trainer**

Name _____

Identify and Name Rectangles

Essential Question How can you identify and name rectangles?

Common Core **Geometry—K.G.A.2**

MATHEMATICAL PRACTICES
MP5, MP6, MP7

rectangles	not rectangles

DIRECTIONS Place two-dimensional shapes on the page. Identify and name the rectangles. Sort the shapes by rectangles and not rectangles. Trace and color the shapes on the sorting mat.

Chapter 9 • Lesson 7

five hundred twenty-nine **529**

1

Name _____

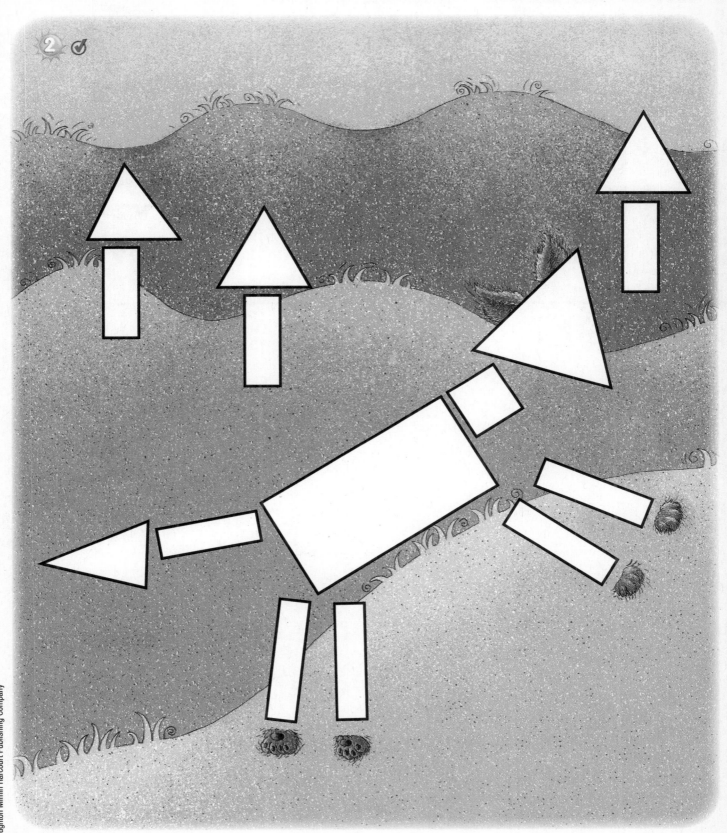

DIRECTIONS 2. Color the rectangles in the picture.

Problem Solving • Applications Real World

3

WRITE Math

4

DIRECTIONS **3.** Max looked at his shapes. Which of his shapes are rectangles? Mark an X on those shapes. **4.** Draw to show what you know about rectangles. Tell a friend about your drawing.

HOME ACTIVITY • Have your child show you an object that is shaped like a rectangle.

Identify and Name Rectangles

Practice and Homework
Lesson 9.7

COMMON CORE STANDARD—K.G.A.2
Identify and describe shapes (squares, circles, triangles, rectangles, hexagons, cubes, cones, cylinders, and spheres).

DIRECTIONS 1. Color the rectangles in the picture.

Spiral Review (K.CC.A.1, K.CC.B.5)

1	2	3	4	5	6	7	8	9	10
11	12	13	14	15	16	17	18	19	20
21	22	23	24	25	26	27	28	29	30

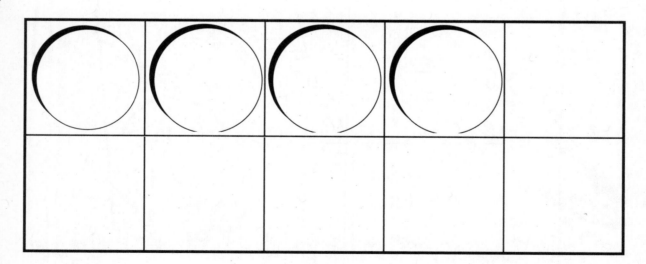

DIRECTIONS 1. Which shape is a rectangle? Color the rectangle.
2. Count by tens as you point to the numbers in the shaded boxes. Start
with the number 10. What number do you end with? Draw a line under
that number. 3. How many more counters would you place to model a
way to make 6? Draw the counters.

534 five hundred thirty-four

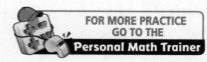

FOR MORE PRACTICE
GO TO THE
Personal Math Trainer

Name _____

Describe Rectangles

Essential Question How can you describe rectangles?

Common Core Geometry—K.G.B.4

MATHEMATICAL PRACTICES
MP2, MP7, MP8

Listen and Draw

side

vertex

© Houghton Mifflin Harcourt Publishing Company

DIRECTIONS Use your finger to trace around the rectangle.
Talk about the number of sides and the number of vertices. Draw
an arrow pointing to another vertex. Trace around the sides.

Chapter 9 • Lesson 8

five hundred thirty-five **535**

rectangle

 _____

 **vertices**

2 _____

_____ **sides**

DIRECTIONS 1. Place a counter on each corner, or vertex. Write how many corners, or vertices. 2. Trace around the sides. Write how many sides.

536 five hundred thirty-six

DIRECTIONS 3. Draw and color a rectangle.

Problem Solving • Applications

4

DIRECTIONS 4. I have 4 sides and 4 vertices. What shape am I? Draw the shape. Tell a friend the name of the shape.

HOME ACTIVITY • Have your child describe a rectangle.

538 five hundred thirty-eight

Describe Rectangles

 COMMON CORE STANDARD—K.G.B.4
Analyze, compare, create, and compose shapes.

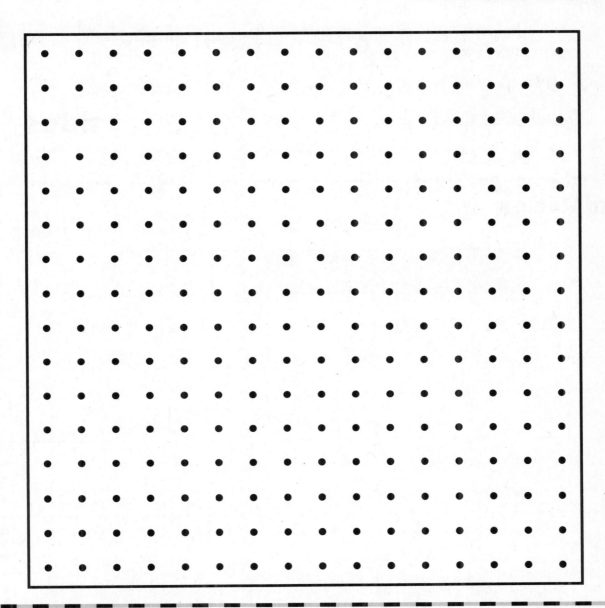

_____

- - - - -

_____ **vertices**

_____

- - - - -

_____ **sides**

DIRECTIONS **I.** Draw and color a rectangle.   **2.** Place a counter on each corner, or vertex, of the rectangle that you drew. Write how many corners, or vertices.   **3.** Trace around the sides of the rectangle that you drew. Write how many sides.

Lesson Check (K.G.B.4)

_____

- - - - - - - - - -

_____ **sides**

Spiral Review (K.CC.A.3, K.OA.A.2)

_____   +   _____   =   _____

- - - - - - - - - - - - -

_____

_____

DIRECTIONS **I.** How many sides does the rectangle have? Write the number. **2.** Complete the addition sentence to show the numbers that match the cube train. **3.** Draw a set that has 20 connecting cubes. Write the number.

**FOR MORE PRACTICE
GO TO THE
Personal Math Trainer**

Name _____

Identify and Name Hexagons

Essential Question How can you identify and name hexagons?

Common Core Geometry—K.G.A.2

MATHEMATICAL PRACTICES
MP5, MP6, MP7

hexagons	not hexagons

DIRECTIONS Place two-dimensional shapes on the page. Identify and name the hexagons. Sort the shapes by hexagons and not hexagons. Trace and color the shapes on the sorting mat.

Chapter 9 • Lesson 9

five hundred forty-one **541**

1

DIRECTIONS 1. Mark an X on all of the hexagons.

Name _____

DIRECTIONS 2. Color the hexagons in the picture.

Problem Solving • Applications Real World

③   WRITE Math

❀

DIRECTIONS 3. Ryan is looking at his shapes. Which of his shapes are hexagons? Mark an X on those shapes.   4. Draw to show what you know about hexagons. Tell a friend about your drawing.

HOME ACTIVITY • Draw some shapes on a page. Include several hexagons. Have your child circle the hexagons.

Identify and Name Hexagons

COMMON CORE STANDARD—K.G.A.2
*Identify and describe shapes (squares, circles,
triangles, rectangles, hexagons, cubes, cones,
cylinders, and spheres).*

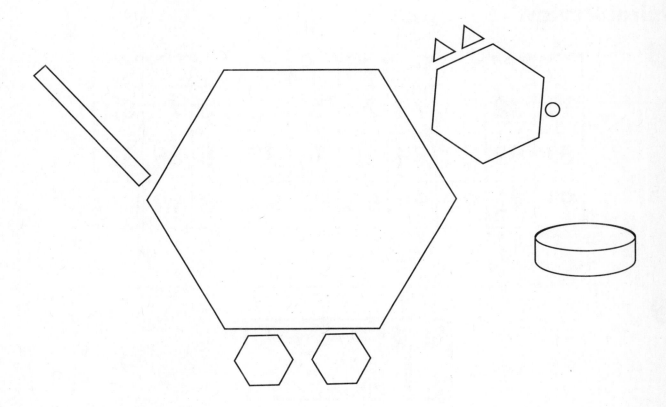

DIRECTIONS 1. Color the hexagons in the picture.

Lesson Check (K.G.A.2)

 1

Spiral Review (K.CC.A.1, K.OA.A.1)

 2

71	72	73	74	75	76	77	78	79	80
81	82	83	84	85	86	87	88	89	90
91	92	93	94	95	96	97	98	99	100

3

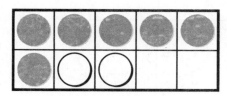

‒ ‒ ‒ ‒ ‒   +   ‒ ‒ ‒ ‒ ‒

DIRECTIONS 1. Which shape is a hexagon? Color the hexagon.
2. Begin with 81 and count forward to 90. What is the next number?
Draw a line under that number. **3.** What numbers show the sets that
are put together? Write the numbers and trace the symbol.

**FOR MORE PRACTICE
GO TO THE
Personal Math Trainer**

Name _____

Describe Hexagons

Essential Question How can you describe hexagons?

Common Core Geometry—K.G.B.4

MATHEMATICAL PRACTICES
MP2, MP7, MP8

Listen and Draw

vertex

side

DIRECTIONS Use your finger to trace around the hexagon.
Talk about the number of sides and the number of vertices. Draw
an arrow pointing to another vertex. Trace around the sides.

Chapter 9 • Lesson 10

five hundred forty-seven **547**

hexagon

1 ☑

_____ vertices

2 ☑

_____ sides

DIRECTIONS 1. Place a counter on each corner, or vertex. Write how many corners, or vertices. 2. Trace around the sides. Write how many sides.

③

DIRECTIONS 3. Draw and color a hexagon.

Problem Solving • Applications

4

DIRECTIONS 4. I have 6 sides and 6 vertices. What shape am I? Draw the shape. Tell a friend the name of the shape.

HOME ACTIVITY • Have your child describe a hexagon.

Describe Hexagons

Common Core **COMMON CORE STANDARD—K.G.B.4**
Analyze, compare, create, and compose shapes.

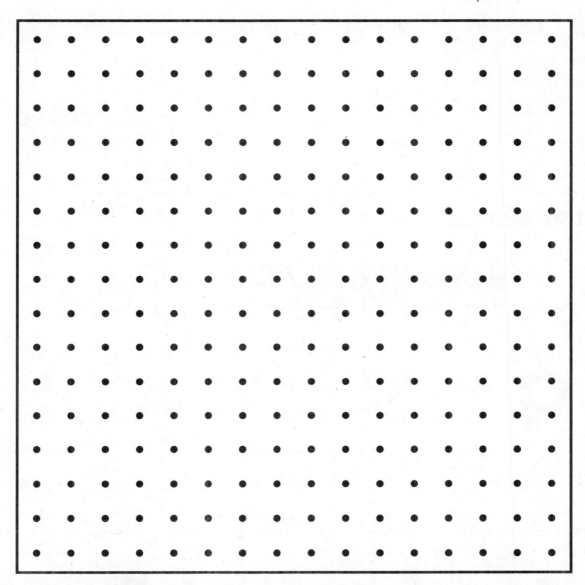

2 _____
    - - - - - - -
    _____ **vertices**

3 _____
    - - - - - - -
    _____ **sides**

DIRECTIONS 1. Draw and color a hexagon. 2. Place a counter on each corner, or vertex, of the hexagon that you drew. Write how many corners, or vertices. 3. Trace around the sides of the hexagon that you drew. Write how many sides.

Chapter 9

Lesson Check (K.G.B.4)

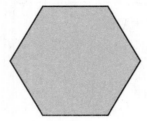

_____

- - - - - - -

_____ sides

Spiral Review (K.CC.C.7, K.OA.A.3)

9 === - - - - - + - - - -

6   **7**

DIRECTIONS 1. How many sides does the hexagon have? Write the number. 2. Complete the addition sentence to show the numbers that match the cube train. 3. Compare the numbers. Circle the number that is greater.

552 five hundred fifty-two

 **FOR MORE PRACTICE GO TO THE Personal Math Trainer**

Name _____

Algebra • Compare Two-Dimensional Shapes

Essential Question How can you use the words *alike* and *different* to compare two-dimensional shapes?

Common Core Geometry—K.G.B.4

MATHEMATICAL PRACTICES
MP5, MP7, MP8

Listen and Draw

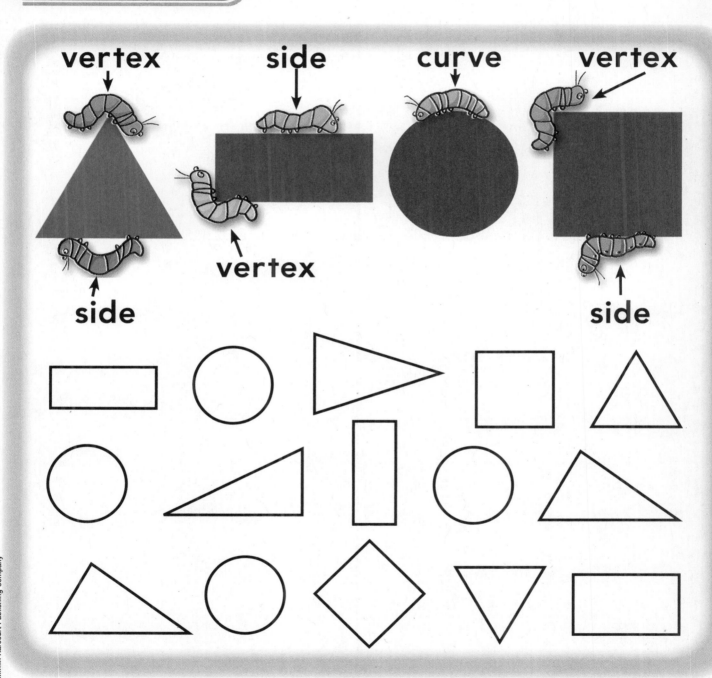

DIRECTIONS Look at the worms and the shapes. Use the words *alike* and *different* to compare the shapes. Use green to color the shapes with four vertices and four sides. Use blue to color the shapes with curves. Use red to color the shapes with three vertices and three sides.

Chapter 9 • Lesson 11

five hundred fifty-three **553**

alike	different

DIRECTIONS 1. Place two-dimensional shapes on the page. Sort the shapes by the number of vertices. Draw the shapes on the sorting mat. Use the words *alike* and *different* to tell how you sorted the shapes.

Name _____

alike	different

DIRECTIONS 2. Place two-dimensional shapes on the page. Sort the shapes by the number of sides. Draw the shapes on the sorting mat. Use the words *alike* and *different* to tell how you sorted the shapes.

Problem Solving • Applications

WRITE Math

3

 4

curve	no curve

DIRECTIONS **3.** I have a curve. What shape am I? Draw the shape. **4.** Draw to show shapes sorted by curves and no curves.

 HOME ACTIVITY • Describe a shape and ask your child to name the shape that you are describing.

Algebra • Compare Two-Dimensional Shapes

COMMON CORE STANDARD—K.G.B.4
Analyze, compare, create, and compose shapes.

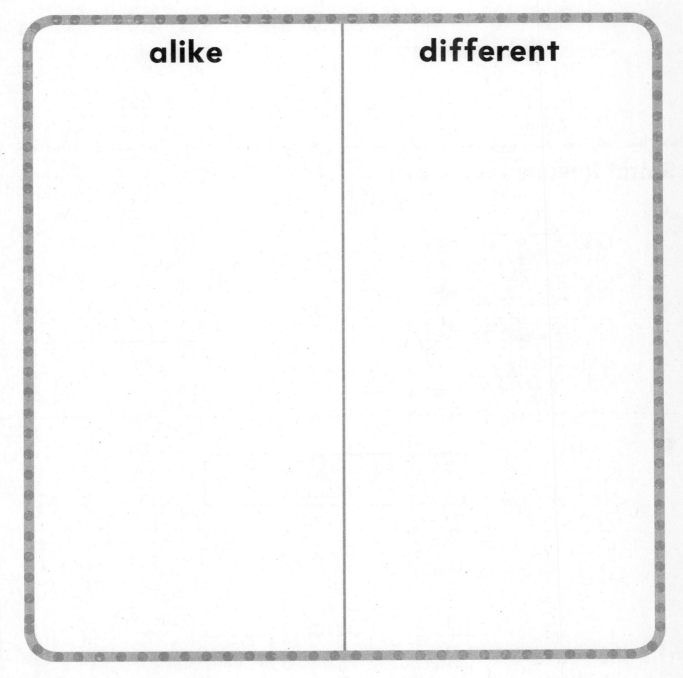

alike	different

DIRECTIONS I. Place two-dimensional shapes on the page. Sort the shapes by the number of sides. Draw the shapes on the sorting mat. Use the words *alike* and *different* to tell how you sorted the shapes.

Lesson Check (K.G.B.4)

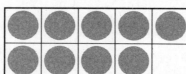

Spiral Review (K.OA.A.1, K.NBT.A.1)

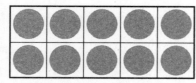

and _____

DIRECTIONS 1. Look at the shape. Draw a shape that is alike in some way. Tell how the two shapes are alike. 2. Count and tell how many. Write the number. 3. How many of each color counter? Write the numbers.

FOR MORE PRACTICE
GO TO THE
Personal Math Trainer

Name _____

Problem Solving • Draw to Join Shapes

Essential Question How can you solve problems using the strategy *draw a picture*?

Common Core Geometry—K.G.B.6

MATHEMATICAL PRACTICES
MP5, MP7, MP8

Unlock the Problem

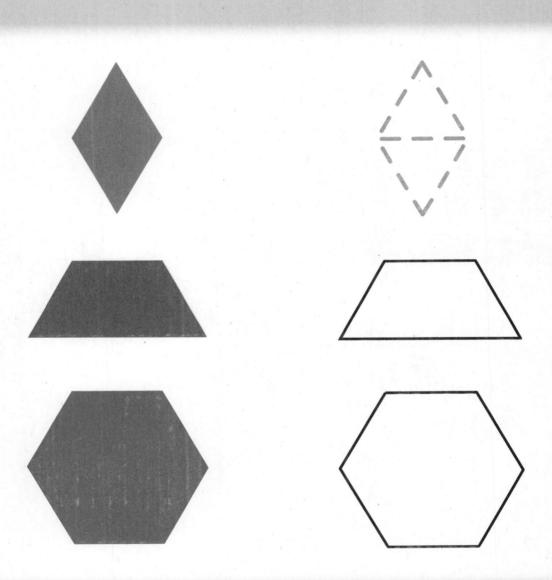

© Houghton Mifflin Harcourt Publishing Company

DIRECTIONS How can you join triangles to make the shapes? Draw and color the triangles.

DIRECTIONS 1. How can you join the two triangles to make a rectangle? Trace around the triangles to draw the rectangle. 2. How can you join the two triangles to make a larger triangle? Use the triangle shapes to draw a larger triangle.

Share and Show

3

4 ✓

DIRECTIONS **3.** How can you join some of the squares to make a larger square? Use the square shapes to draw a larger square. **4.** How can you join some or all of the squares to make a rectangle? Use the square shapes to draw a rectangle.

Chapter 9 • Lesson 12   five hundred sixty-one **561**

On Your Own

5

WRITE
Math

6

DIRECTIONS 5. Can you join these shapes to make a hexagon? Use the shapes to draw a hexagon. 6. Which shapes could you join to make a larger shape that looks like a flower? Draw and color to show the shapes you used.

HOME ACTIVITY • Have your child join shapes to form a larger shape, and then tell you about the shape.

Problem Solving • Draw to Join Shapes

Common Core **COMMON CORE STANDARD—K.G.B.6**
Analyze, compare, create, and compose shapes.

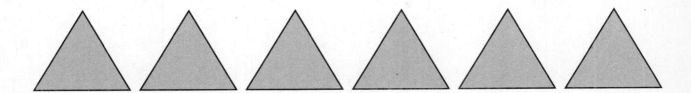

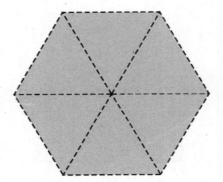

DIRECTIONS 1. Place triangles on the page as shown. How can you join all of the triangles to make a hexagon? Trace around the triangles to draw the hexagon. **2.** How can you join some of the triangles to make a larger triangle? Trace around the triangles to draw the larger triangle.

Lesson Check (K.G.B.6)

Spiral Review (K.CC.B.5, K.CC.C.6)

②

_____

- - - - - - - - - - - - - -

_____

③

_____   _____

- - - - - - - - - -   - - - - - - - - - -

_____   _____

DIRECTIONS **1.** Join two triangles to make a shape. Draw and color the triangles you used. **2.** Count and tell how many. Write the number. **3.** Count and tell how many in each set. Write the numbers. Compare the numbers. Circle the number that is less.

**FOR MORE PRACTICE
GO TO THE
Personal Math Trainer**

Chapter 9 Review/Test

○ Yes   ○ No

○ Yes   ○ No

○ Yes   ○ No

○   ○   ○   ○

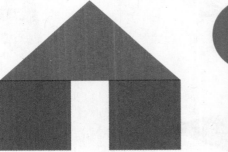 

_____
_ _ _ _ _ _
_____ **squares**

© Houghton Mifflin Harcourt Publishing Company

DIRECTIONS 1. Is the shape a circle? Choose Yes or No. 2. Mark under all the shapes that have curves. 3. How many squares are in the picture? Write the number.

Chapter 9

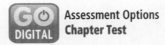 **Assessment Options
Chapter Test**

4

_____

- - - - - -

_____ sides

5

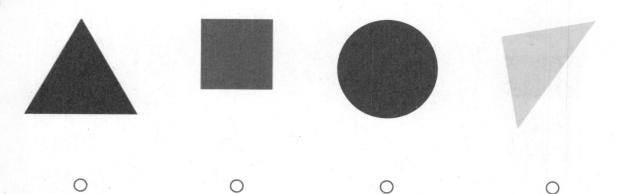

○   ○   ○   ○

Personal Math Trainer

6 THINK SMARTER +

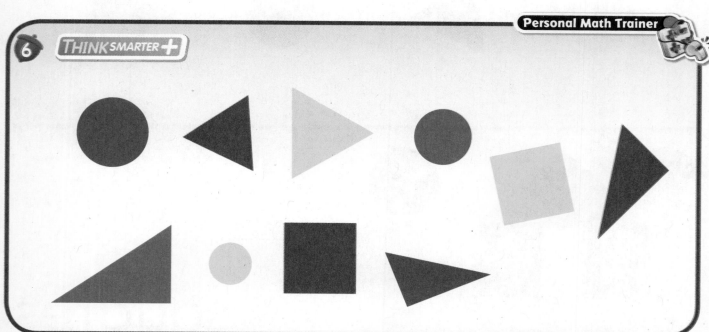

DIRECTIONS **4.** Look at the square. Write the number of sides on a square. **5.** Mark under all of the shapes that are triangles. **6.** Mark an X on each shape that has 3 sides and 3 vertices.

566 five hundred sixty-six

Name _____

 7

8 THINK SMARTER +

Personal Math Trainer

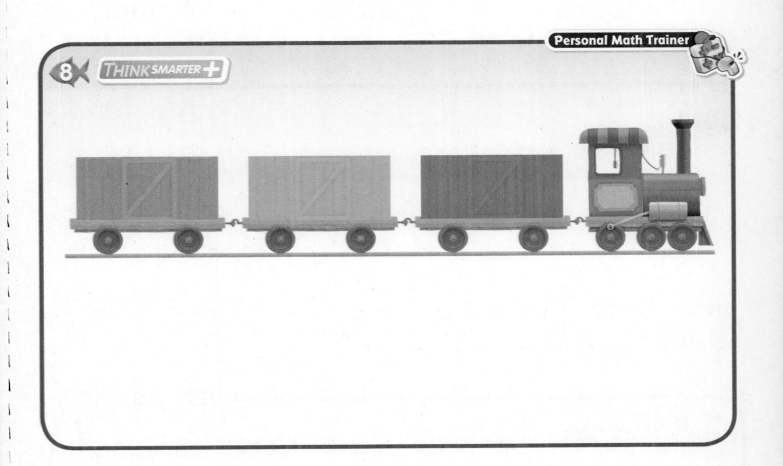

9

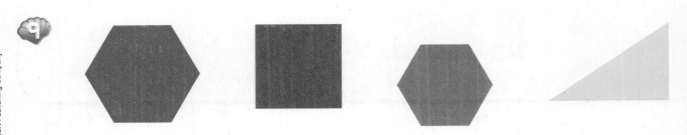

DIRECTIONS **7.** Mark an X on the shape that is not a
rectangle. **8.** Draw a shape that is the same as the boxcars on the
train. **9.** Mark an X on all of the hexagons.

Chapter 9

4 sides   3 sides   6 sides

11

12 THINK SMARTER +

DIRECTIONS 10. Match the shape to the number with that many sides. 11. Look at the shapes. Compare them to see how they are alike and how they are different. Use red to color the shapes with four sides. Use green to color the shapes with curves. Use blue to color the shapes with three vertices. 12. Join shapes to make an arrow. Draw the arrow.

568 five hundred sixty-eight

Identify and Describe Three-Dimensional Shapes

Curious About Math with **Curious George**

Many of the shapes in our environment are three-dimensional shapes.

Name some of the shapes you see in this picture.

Name _____

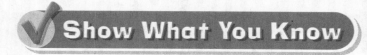 

Identify Shapes

 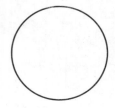 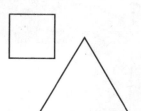 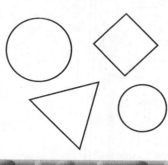

Describe Shapes

 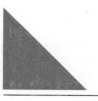

_____

_____ sides

_____ vertices

_____

_____ sides

_____ vertices

Sort Shapes

This page checks understanding of important skills needed for success in Chapter 10.

DIRECTIONS 1. Use red to color the squares. Use blue to color the triangles. 2–3. Look at the shape. Write how many sides. Write how many vertices. 4. Mark an X on the shapes with three sides.

570 five hundred seventy

Name _____

Vocabulary Builder

rectangle

circle

square

triangle

DIRECTIONS Mark an X on the food shaped like a circle. Draw a line under the food shaped like a square. Circle the food shaped like a triangle.

GO DIGITAL
- **Interactive Student Edition**
- **Multimedia eGlossary**

Game

Follow the Shapes

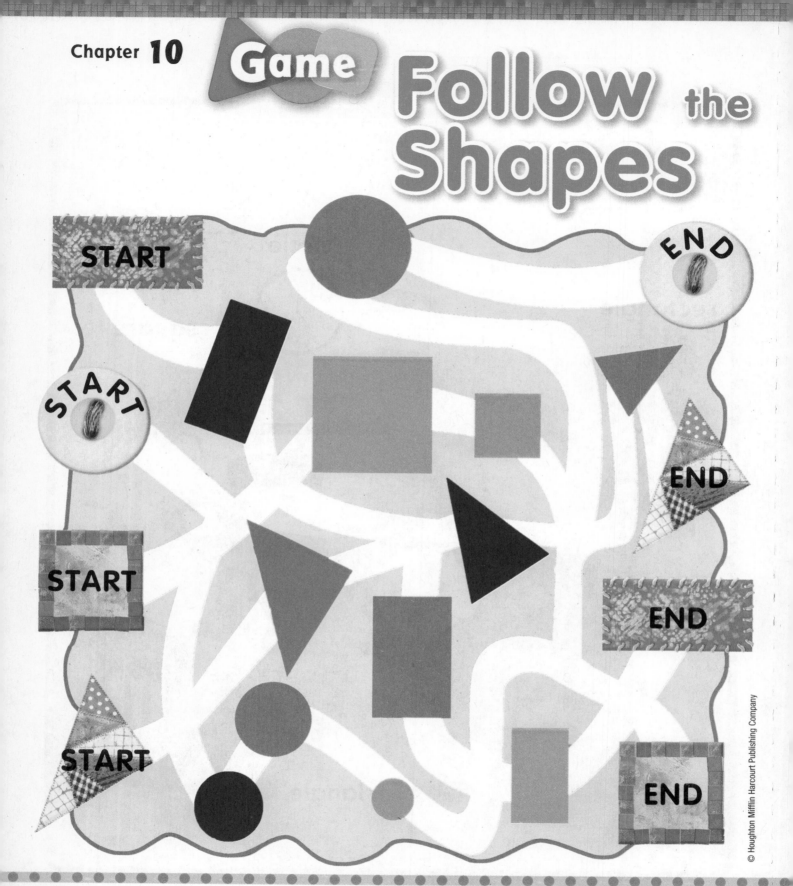

DIRECTIONS Choose a shape from START. Follow the path that has the same shapes. Draw a line to show the path to the END with the same shape.

Chapter 10 Vocabulary

above

arriba, encima

1

behind

detrás

5

below

debajo

6

beside

al lado

7

cone

cono

14

cube

cubo

15

curved surface

superficie curva

17

cylinder

cilindro

18

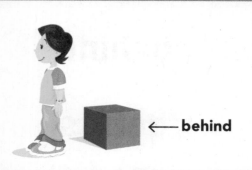 ← **behind**

 ← **above**

The flowers are **beside** the tree.

below →

cube

cone

cylinder

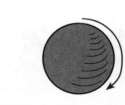 **curved surface**

flat surface

superficie plana

27

in front of

delante de

35

next to

al lado de

44

roll

rodar

54

slide

deslizar

67

sphere

esfera

69

stack

apilar

71

three-dimensional shapes

figuras tridimensionales

78

in front of →

flat surface

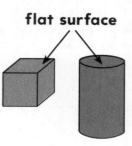

roll

The flowers are **next to** the tree.

sphere

slide →

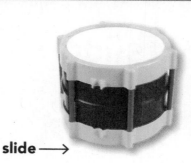

three-dimensional shapes

The cubes **stack** on top of one another.

Game

Picture It

Word Box

above
behind
below
beside
next to
in front of
cone
cube

Word Box

curved surface
cylinder
flat surface
roll
slide
sphere
stack
three-dimensional shape

Secret Words

Player 1					
Player 2					

DIRECTIONS Players take turns. A player chooses a secret word from the Word Box and then sets the timer. The player draws pictures to give hints about the secret word. If the other player guesses the secret word before time runs out, he or she puts a counter in the chart. The first player who has counters in all his or her boxes is the winner.

MATERIALS timer, drawing paper, two-color counters for each player

The Write Way

DIRECTIONS Choose one idea. • Choose 2 three-dimensional shapes. Draw to show what you know about the shapes. • Draw to show *above*, *below*, and *next to*.
Reflect Be ready to tell about your drawing.

Name _____

Three-Dimensional Shapes

Essential Question How can you show which shapes stack, roll, or slide?

does stack	does not stack

DIRECTIONS Place three-dimensional shapes on the page. Sort the shapes by whether they stack or do not stack. Describe the shapes. Match a picture of each shape to the shapes on the sorting mat. Glue the shape pictures on the sorting mat.

Chapter 10 • Lesson 1

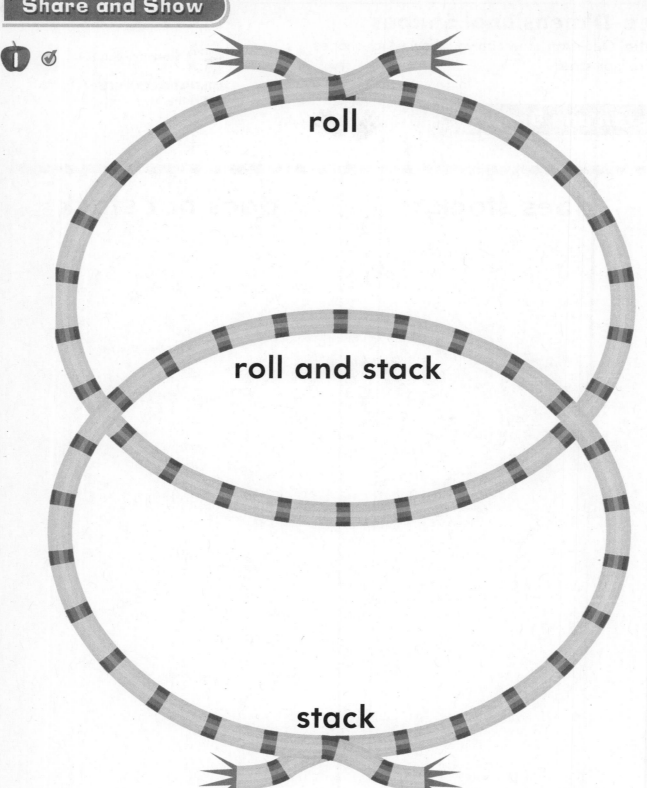

roll

roll and stack

stack

DIRECTIONS 1. Place three-dimensional shapes on the page. Sort the shapes by whether they roll, roll and stack, or stack. Describe the shapes. Match a picture of each shape to the shapes. Glue the shape pictures on the page.

Name _____

2

roll

3

stack

4

slide

5

stack and slide

DIRECTIONS **2.** Which shape does not roll? Mark an X on that shape.
3. Which shapes do not stack? Mark an X on those shapes. **4.** Which shape does not slide? Mark an X on that shape. **5.** Which shape does not stack and slide? Mark an X on that shape.

Problem Solving • Applications Real World

6

7

DIRECTIONS 6. I roll and do not stack. Describe the shape. Mark an X on that shape. **7.** Draw to show what you know about a real object that rolls and does not stack.

HOME ACTIVITY • Have your child identify and describe an object in the house that rolls and does not stack.

576 five hundred seventy-six

Three-Dimensional Shapes

 COMMON CORE STANDARD—K.G.B.4
Analyze, compare, create, and compose shapes.

 ①

roll

---

 ②

stack

---

 ③

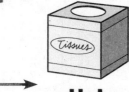
slide

---

 ④

stack and slide

DIRECTIONS **1.** Which shape does not roll? Mark an X on that shape. **2.** Which shapes do not stack? Mark an X on those shapes. **3.** Which shape does not slide? Mark an X on that shape. **4.** Which shape does not stack and slide? Mark an X on that shape.

Spiral Review (K.CC.A.2, K.G.B.4)

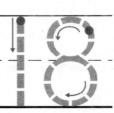

DIRECTIONS 1. Which shape does not roll? Mark an X on the shape. 2. Count forward. Trace and write the numbers in order. 3. Which shape has a curve? Color the shape.

© Houghton Mifflin Harcourt Publishing Company

FOR MORE PRACTICE
GO TO THE
Personal Math Trainer

Name _____

Identify, Name, and Describe Spheres

Essential Question How can you identify, name, and describe spheres?

Common Core Geometry—K.G.A.2

MATHEMATICAL PRACTICES
MP5, MP6, MP7

Listen and Draw Real World

sphere	not a sphere

DIRECTIONS Place three-dimensional shapes on the page. Identify and name the sphere. Sort the shapes on the sorting mat. Describe the sphere. Match a picture of each shape to the shapes on the sorting mat. Glue the shape pictures on the sorting mat.

Chapter 10 • Lesson 2

1

sphere

flat surface

curved surface

2 ✓

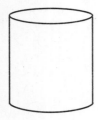   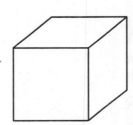

 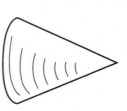 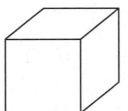 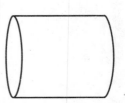

DIRECTIONS 1. Look at the sphere. Circle the words that describe a sphere. 2. Color the spheres.

DIRECTIONS 3. Identify the objects that are shaped like a sphere. Mark an X on those objects.

Chapter 10 • Lesson 2

Problem Solving • Applications Real World

WRITE Math

4

5

DIRECTIONS 4. I have a curved surface. Which shape am I? Mark an X on that shape.   **5.** Draw to show what you know about a real object that is shaped like a sphere.

HOME ACTIVITY • Have your child identify and describe an object in the house that is shaped like a sphere.

Identify, Name, and Describe Spheres

Common Core **COMMON CORE STANDARD—K.G.A.2**
Identify and describe shapes (squares, circles, triangles, rectangles, hexagons, cubes, cones, cylinders, and spheres).

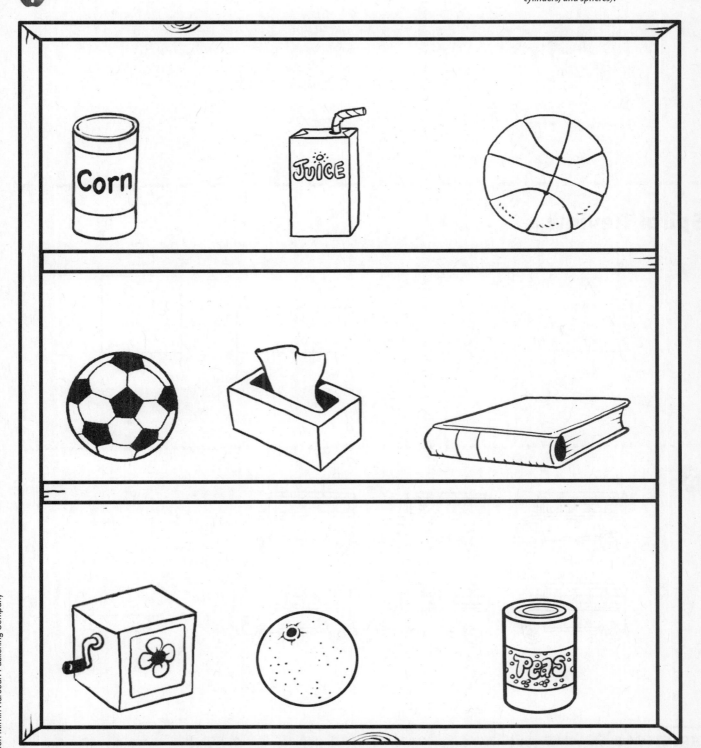

DIRECTIONS 1. Identify the objects that are shaped like a sphere. Mark an X on those objects.

Chapter 10

five hundred eighty-three **583**

Lesson Check (K.G.A.2)

Spiral Review (K.CC.A.3, K.G.A.2)

_____

- - - - -

_____

DIRECTIONS 1. Which shape is a sphere? Mark an X on the shape. 2. Which shape is a square? Color the square. 3. How many school buses are there? Write the number.

Name _____

Identify, Name, and Describe Cubes

Essential Question How can you identify, name, and describe cubes?

Common Core Geometry—K.G.A.2

MATHEMATICAL PRACTICES
MP2, MP5, MP6

Listen and Draw (Real World)   Hands On

cube	not a cube

DIRECTIONS Place three-dimensional shapes on the page. Identify and name the cube. Sort the shapes on the sorting mat. Describe the cube. Match a picture of each shape to the shapes on the sorting mat. Glue the shape pictures on the sorting mat.

cube

flat surface

curved surface

_____

_ _ _ _

_____ flat surfaces

DIRECTIONS 1. Look at the cube. Circle the words that describe a cube.   2. Use a cube to count how many flat surfaces. Write the number.

DIRECTIONS 3. Identify the objects that are shaped like a cube. Mark an X on those objects.

Chapter 10 • Lesson 3

five hundred eighty-seven **587**

Problem Solving • Applications Real World

WRITE Math

❀4

❀5

© Houghton Mifflin Harcourt Publishing Company

DIRECTIONS 4. I have 6 flat surfaces. Which shape am I? Mark an X on that shape. **5.** Draw to show what you know about a real object that is shaped like a cube.

HOME ACTIVITY • Have your child identify and describe an object in the house that is shaped like a cube.

Identify, Name, and Describe Cubes

 COMMON CORE STANDARD—K.G.A.2
*Identify and describe shapes (squares, circles,
triangles, rectangles, hexagons, cubes, cones,
cylinders, and spheres).*

DIRECTIONS 1. Identify the objects that are shaped
like a cube. Mark an X on those objects.

Spiral Review (K.CC.A.1, K.G.B.4)

_____

- - - - - -

_____ **sides**

71	72	73	74	75	76	77	78	79	80
81	82	83	84	85	86	87	88	89	90
91	92	93	94	95	96	97	98	99	100

DIRECTIONS **1.** Which shape is a cube? Mark an X on the shape. **2.** How many sides does the square have? Write the number. **3.** Begin with 81 and count forward to 90. What is the next number? Draw a line under that number.

© Houghton Mifflin Harcourt Publishing Company

FOR MORE PRACTICE GO TO THE
Personal Math Trainer

Name _____

Identify, Name, and Describe Cylinders

Essential Question How can you identify, name, and describe cylinders?

Common Core Geometry—K.G.A.2

MATHEMATICAL PRACTICES
MP2, MP5, MP6

Listen and Draw

cylinder	not a cylinder

DIRECTIONS Place three-dimensional shapes on the page. Identify and name the cylinder. Sort the shapes on the sorting mat. Describe the cylinder. Match a picture of each shape to the shapes on the sorting mat. Glue the shape pictures on the sorting mat.

Chapter 10 • Lesson 4

cylinder

flat surface

curved surface

_____

_ _ _ _ _ _

_____ **flat surfaces**

DIRECTIONS 1. Look at the cylinder. Circle the words that describe a cylinder.
2. Use a cylinder to count how many flat surfaces. Write the number.

DIRECTIONS 3. Identify the objects that are shaped like a cylinder. Mark an X on those objects.

Problem Solving • Applications Real World

4

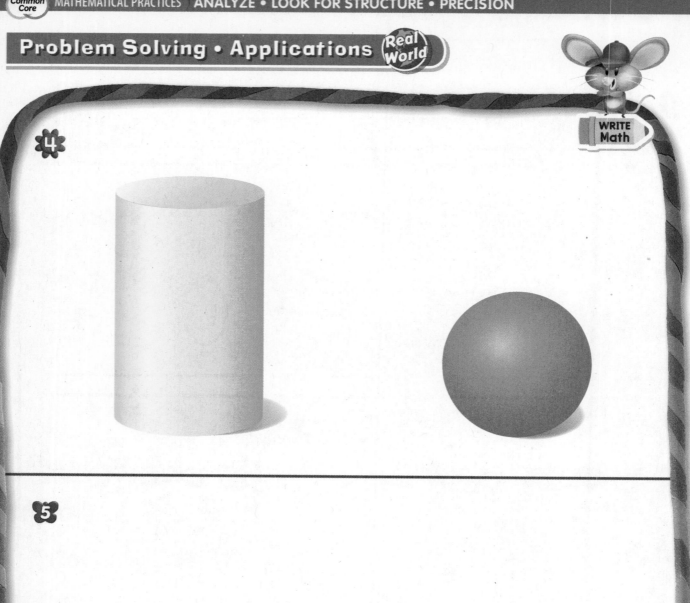

5

DIRECTIONS 4. I have 2 flat surfaces. Which shape am I? Mark an X on that shape. 5. Draw to show what you know about a real object that is shaped like a cylinder.

HOME ACTIVITY • Have your child identify and describe an object in the house that is shaped like a cylinder.

Identify, Name, and Describe Cylinders

COMMON CORE STANDARD—K.G.A.2
Identify and describe shapes (squares, circles, triangles, rectangles, hexagons, cubes, cones, cylinders, and spheres).

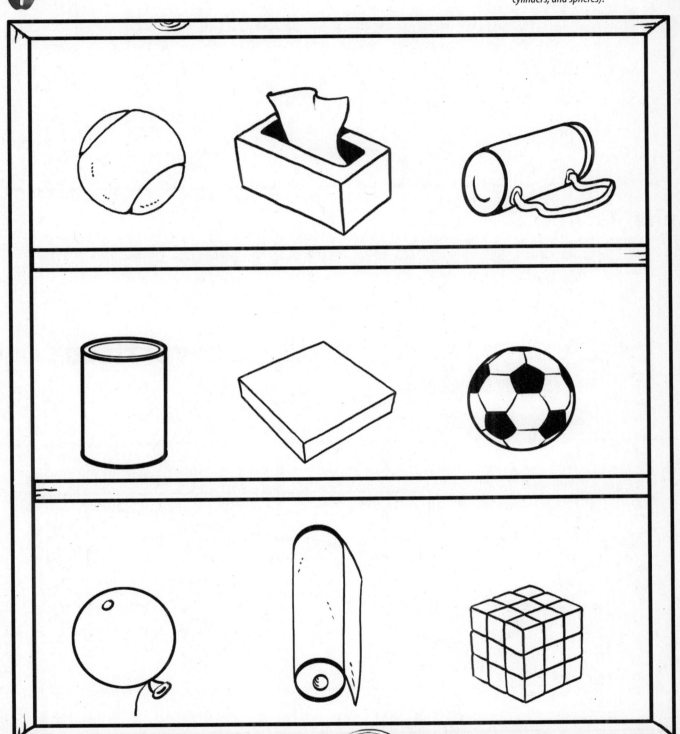

DIRECTIONS 1. Identify the objects that are shaped like a cylinder. Mark an X on those objects.

Lesson Check (K.G.A.2)

Spiral Review (K.OA.A.5, K.G.B.4)

2

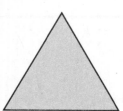

_____

- - - - - -

_____ **vertices**

3

_____

$$5 - \text{-----} = 2$$

_____

DIRECTIONS 1. Which shape is a cylinder? Mark an X on the shape. 2. How many vertices does the triangle have? Write the number. 3. Write the number to show how many are being taken from the set.

© Houghton Mifflin Harcourt Publishing Company

FOR MORE PRACTICE
GO TO THE
Personal Math Trainer

Name _____

Identify, Name, and Describe Cones

Essential Question How can you identify, name, and describe cones?

Common Core Geometry—K.G.A.2

MATHEMATICAL PRACTICES
MP2, MP5, MP6

cone	not a cone

DIRECTIONS Place three-dimensional shapes on the page. Identify and name the cone. Sort the shapes on the sorting mat. Describe the cone. Match a picture of each shape to the shapes on the sorting mat. Glue the shape pictures on the sorting mat.

Chapter 10 • Lesson 5

five hundred ninety-seven **597**

1

cone

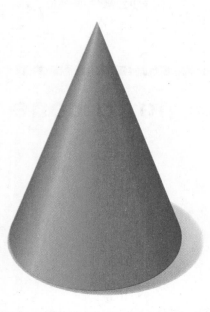

flat surface

curved surface

2 ✓

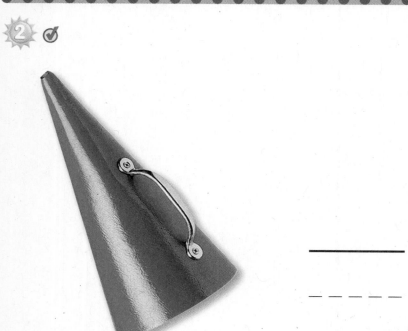

_____

_ _ _ _ _ _

_____ flat surface

DIRECTIONS 1. Look at the cone. Circle the words that describe a cone. 2. Use a cone to count how many flat surfaces. Write the number.

Name _____

DIRECTIONS **3.** Identify the objects that are shaped like a cone. Mark an X on those objects.

HOME ACTIVITY • Have your child identify and describe an object in the house that is shaped like a cone.

Chapter 10 • Lesson 5

five hundred ninety-nine **599**

Concepts and Skills

❶

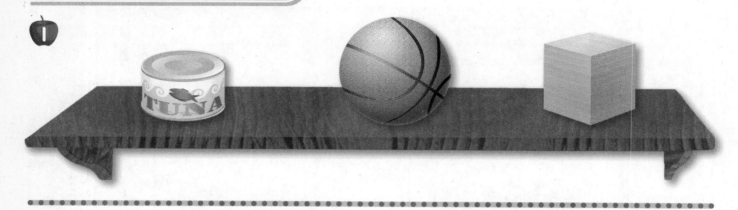

② 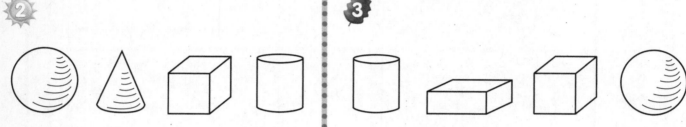 ③

④ THINK SMARTER

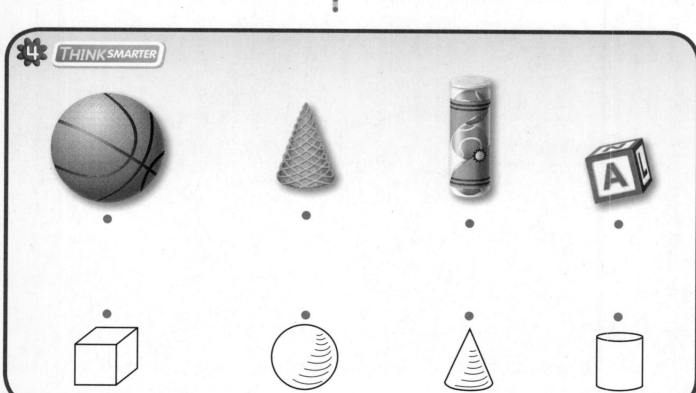

DIRECTIONS 1. Mark an X on the object that is shaped like a cylinder. (K.G.A.2)
2. Color the sphere. (K.G.A.2) **3.** Color the cube. (K.G.A.2) **4.** Draw lines to match the objects to their shapes. (K.G.A.2)

600 six hundred

Identify, Name, and Describe Cones

COMMON CORE STANDARD—K.G.A.2
Identify and describe shapes (squares, circles, triangles, rectangles, hexagons, cubes, cones, cylinders, and spheres).

1

DIRECTIONS 1. Identify the objects that are shaped like a cone. Mark an X on those objects.

Chapter 10

six hundred one **601**

Lesson Check (K.G.A.2)

Spiral Review (K.NBT.A.1, K.G.A.2)

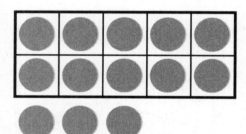

_____

- - - - - - - - - - -

_____

DIRECTIONS 1. Which shape is a cone? Mark an X on the shape. 2. Count and tell how many. Write the number. 3. Which shape is a circle? Color the circle.

602 six hundred two

FOR MORE PRACTICE
GO TO THE
Personal Math Trainer

Problem Solving • Two- and Three-Dimensional Shapes

Essential Question How can you solve problems using the strategy *use logical reasoning*?

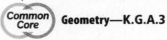

Common Core Geometry—K.G.A.3

MATHEMATICAL PRACTICES
MP4, MP5, MP7

 Unlock the Problem **Real World**

two-dimensional shapes	three-dimensional shapes

DIRECTIONS Place shapes on the page. Sort the shapes on the sorting mat into sets of two-dimensional and three-dimensional shapes. Match a picture of each shape to a shape on the sorting mat. Glue the shape pictures on the sorting mat.

Chapter 10 • Lesson 6

1

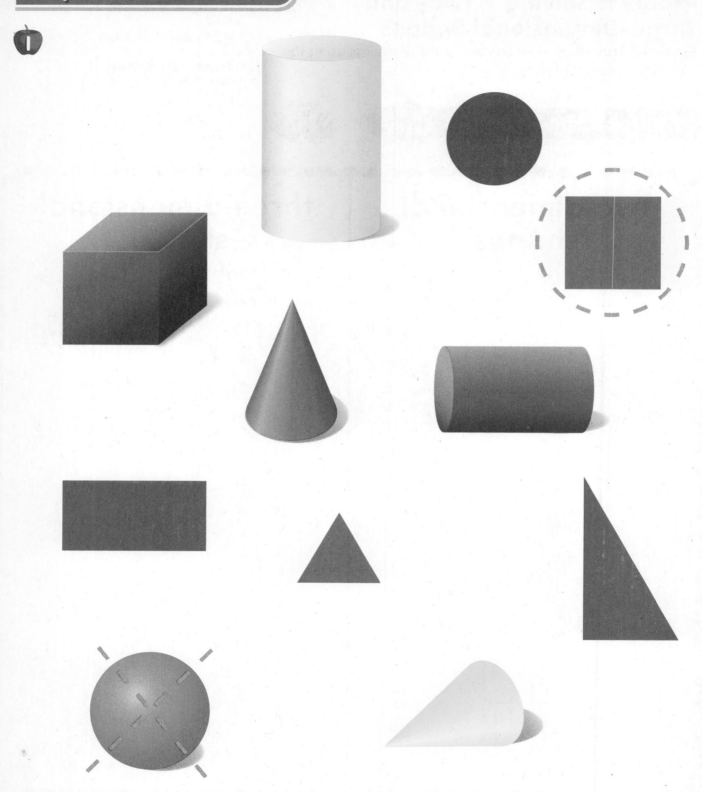

DIRECTIONS 1. Identify the two-dimensional or flat shapes. Trace the circle around the square. Circle the other flat shapes. Identify the three-dimensional or solid shapes. Trace the X on the sphere. Mark an X on the other solid shapes.

Share and Show

 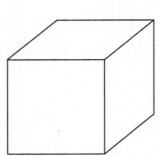

 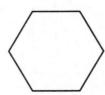 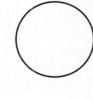

 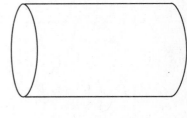

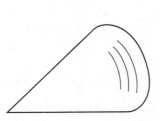 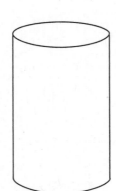 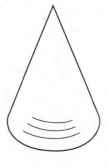

DIRECTIONS 2. Identify the two-dimensional or flat shapes.
Use red to color the flat shapes. Identify the three-dimensional
or solid shapes. Use blue to color the solid shapes.

Chapter 10 • Lesson 6

On Your Own Real World

WRITE Math

3

4

DIRECTIONS **3.** Draw to show what you know about a flat shape. Name the shape. **4.** Draw to show what you know about a real object that has a solid shape. Name the object and the shape.

HOME ACTIVITY • Have your child identify a household object that is shaped like a three-dimensional shape. Have him or her name the three-dimensional shape.

606 six hundred six

Problem Solving • Two- and Three-Dimensional Shapes

Common Core **COMMON CORE STANDARD—K.G.A.3**
*Identify and describe shapes (squares, circles,
triangles, rectangles, hexagons, cubes, cones,
cylinders, and spheres).*

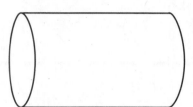
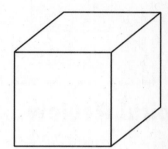

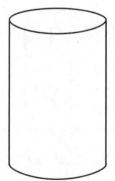
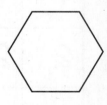

DIRECTIONS 1. Identify the two-dimensional or flat shapes.
Use red to color the flat shapes. Identify the three-dimensional or
solid shapes. Use blue to color the solid shapes.

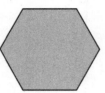

1	2	3	4	5	6	7	8	9	10
11	12	13	14	15	16	17	18	19	20
21	22	23	24	25	26	27	28	29	30

DIRECTIONS 1. Which is a three-dimensional or solid shape? Mark an X on the shape. **2.** Join two triangles to make a shape. Draw and color the shape you created. **3.** Begin with 1 and count forward to 19. What is the next number? Draw a line under that number.

FOR MORE PRACTICE
GO TO THE
Personal Math Trainer

Name _____

Model Shapes

Essential Question How can you model shapes in the real world?

Common Core — **Geometry—K.G.B.5**
Also K.G.A.2, K.G.A.3
MATHEMATICAL PRACTICES
MP3, MP8

Listen and Draw Real World 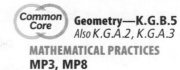 Hands On

DIRECTIONS Use your finger to trace around the shape. Name the shape. Tell a friend whether this shape is flat or solid. Talk about the number of sides and the number of vertices.

Chapter 10 • Lesson 7

six hundred nine **609**

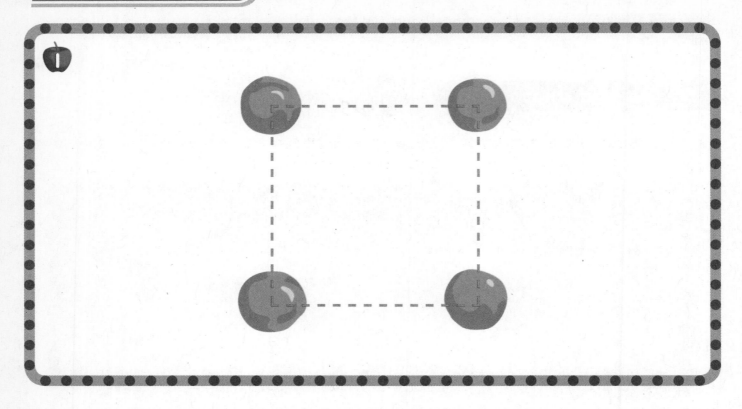

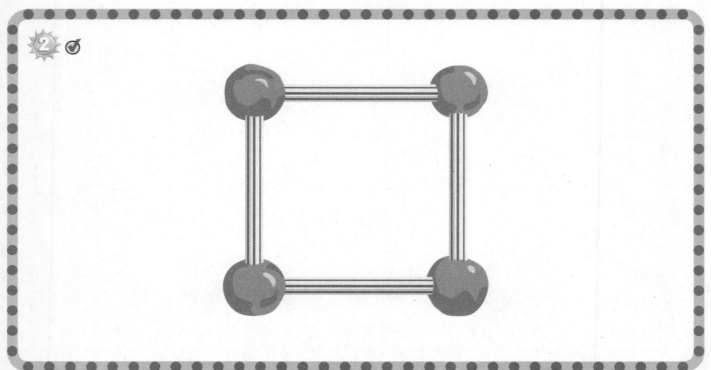

DIRECTIONS 1. Use clay to model 4 spheres as shown. Trace the square. The clay spheres will model the corners of the squares. 2. Place straws into the spheres as shown.

3

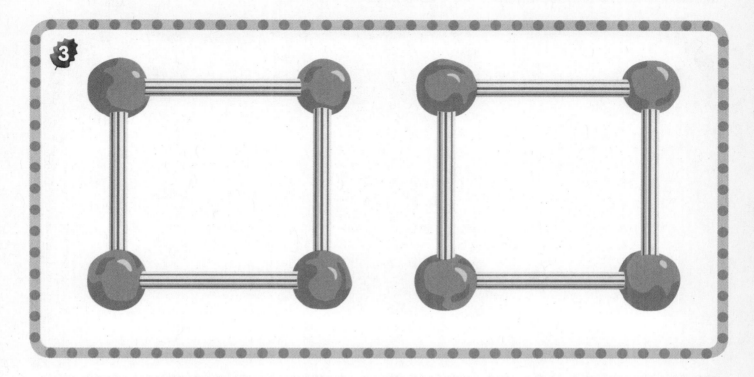

4

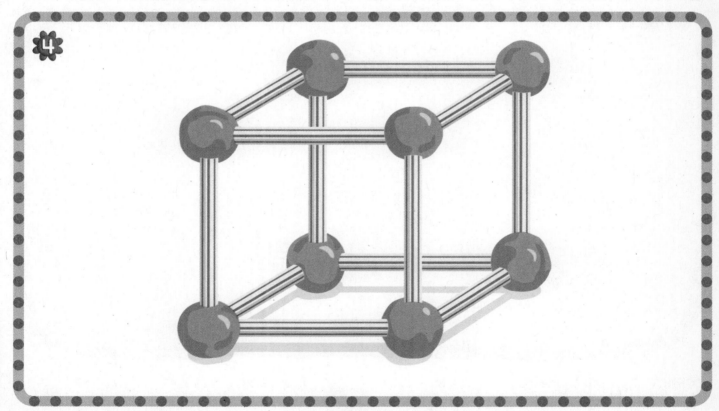

DIRECTIONS 3. Use clay and straws to model another shape. Match the shape that you modeled in Exercise 2. **4.** Stand a straw into each corner of one of the shapes. Carefully lift the other shape and place it onto the straws as shown. Name the solid shape you modeled.

© Houghton Mifflin Harcourt Publishing Company

Problem Solving • Applications

5

6

DIRECTIONS **5.** Maria's window has the shape of a square. Draw a picture of the shape. Tell a friend whether this shape is flat or solid. Talk about the number of sides and the number of vertices. **6.** Use objects such as clay and straws to model a solid shape. Draw a picture of the solid shape. Tell a friend about the shape.

HOME ACTIVITY • Have your child identify a household object that has a flat shape. Have your child model the shape with a drawing. Repeat the activity with a solid object, and have your child model the shape with materials such as clay and toothpicks.

612 six hundred twelve

Model Shapes

Common Core   **COMMON CORE STANDARD—K.G.B.5**
*Model shapes in the world by building shapes
from components (e.g., sticks and clay balls)
and drawing shapes.*

1

_____

_ _ _ _ _ _

_____ **sides**

- -

2

_____

_ _ _ _ _ _

_____ **flat surfaces**

DIRECTIONS 1. Draw to show what you know about a square. Write how many
sides. **2.** Declan's can of corn has the shape of a cylinder. Use clay to model
a cylinder. Draw the cylinder. How many flat surfaces are there? Write the number.

_____

- - - - - - -

_____ **flat surface**

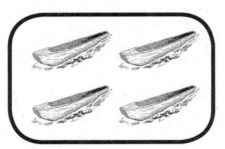

4 + _____ = 5

DIRECTIONS 1. How many flat surfaces does this shape have? Write the number. 2. Which shape is flat? Color the flat shape. 3. Tell an addition word problem about the boats. Write the number to complete the addition sentence.

614 six hundred fourteen

© Houghton Mifflin Harcourt Publishing Company

Name _____

Above and Below

Essential Question How can you use the terms *above* and *below* to describe shapes in the environment?

Common Core Geometry—K.G.A.1

MATHEMATICAL PRACTICES
MP4

Listen and Draw (Real World)

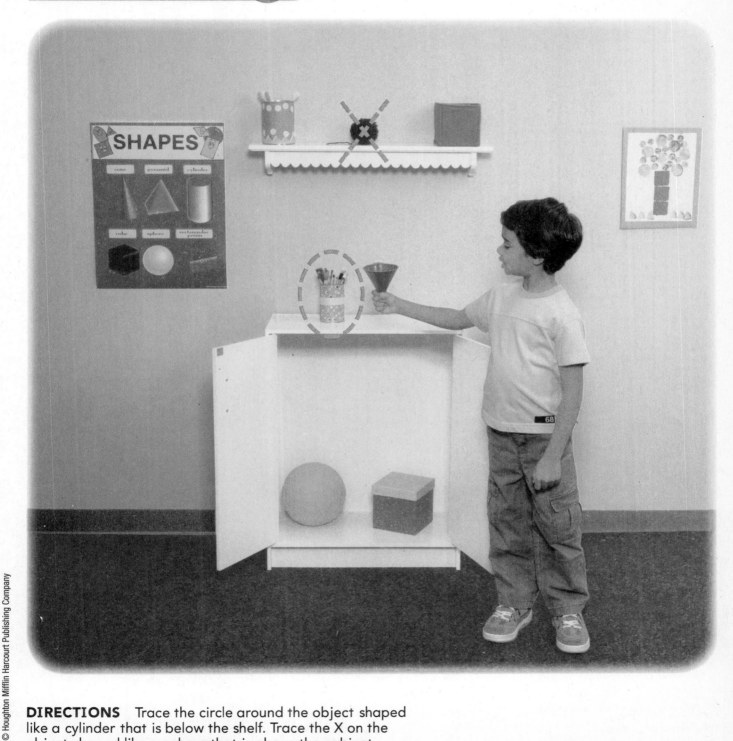

DIRECTIONS Trace the circle around the object shaped like a cylinder that is below the shelf. Trace the X on the object shaped like a sphere that is above the cabinet.

Chapter 10 • Lesson 8

six hundred fifteen **615**

DIRECTIONS 1. Circle the object that is shaped like a cone below the play set. Mark an X on the object that is shaped like a cube above the play set. Color the object that is shaped like a cylinder above the play set.

DIRECTIONS **2.** Circle the object shaped like a sphere above the net. Mark an X on the object shaped like a cube directly below the net.

Problem Solving • Applications

3

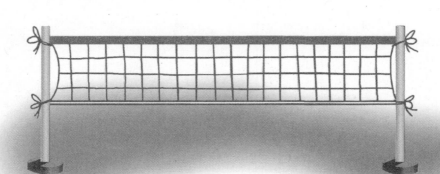

DIRECTIONS 3. Draw to show what you know about real world three-dimensional objects that might be above or below the net. Tell a friend about your drawing as you name the shape of the objects.

 HOME ACTIVITY • Tell your child you are thinking of something in the room that is above or below another object. Have your child tell you what the object might be.

Above and Below

COMMON CORE STANDARD—K.G.A.1
Identify and describe shapes (squares, circles, triangles, rectangles, hexagons, cubes, cones, cylinders, and spheres).

DIRECTIONS I. Mark an X on the object that is shaped like a sphere below the table. Circle the object that is shaped like a cube above the table.

Lesson Check (K.G.A.1)

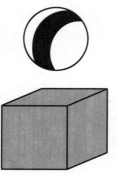

Spiral Review (K.CC.B.5, K.G.B.4)

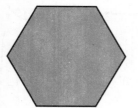

_____

- - - - - - - - -

_____

_____

- - - - - - -

_____ **vertices**

DIRECTIONS 1. Circle the set that shows an object shaped like a sphere above the object shaped like a cube. 2. Count and tell how many. Write the number. 3. How many vertices does the hexagon have? Write the number.

620 six hundred twenty

**FOR MORE PRACTICE
GO TO THE
Personal Math Trainer**

Name _____

Beside and Next To

Essential Question How can you use the terms *beside* and *next to* to describe shapes in the environment?

Common Core   Geometry—K.G.A.1

MATHEMATICAL PRACTICES
MP3, MP4, MP6

DIRECTIONS Trace the X on the object shaped like a cone that is beside the object shaped like a sphere. Trace the circle around the object shaped like a sphere that is next to the object shaped like a cube.

Chapter 10 • Lesson 9

1

DIRECTIONS 1. Mark an X on the bead shaped like a cube that is beside the bead shaped like a cone. Draw a circle around the bead shaped like a cone that is next to the bead shaped like a cylinder. Use the words *next to* and *beside* to name the position of other bead shapes.

Name _____

DIRECTIONS 2. Mark an X on the object shaped like a cylinder that is next to the object shaped like a sphere. Draw a circle around the object shaped like a cone that is beside the object shaped like a cube. Use the words *next to* and *beside* to describe the position of other package shapes.

Chapter 10 • Lesson 9

six hundred twenty-three **623**

Problem Solving • Applications

3

DIRECTIONS 3. Draw or use pictures to show what you know about real world three-dimensional objects beside and next to other objects.

HOME ACTIVITY • Tell your child you are thinking of something in the room that is beside or next to another object. Have your child tell you the shape of the object.

Beside and Next To

Common Core

COMMON CORE STANDARD—K.G.A.1
Identify and describe shapes (squares, circles, triangles, rectangles, hexagons, cubes, cones, cylinders, and spheres).

DIRECTIONS 1. Mark an X on the object shaped like a cylinder that is next to the object shaped like a sphere. Circle the object shaped like a cone that is beside the object shaped like a cube. Use the words *next to* and *beside* to name the position of other shapes.

Chapter 10

Lesson Check (K.G.A.1)

Spiral Review (K.CC.A.3, K.G.A.2)

 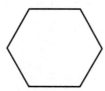

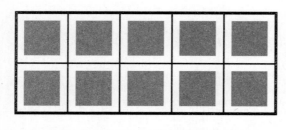

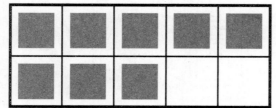

_____

— — — — — — —

_____

DIRECTIONS 1. Circle the set that shows an object shaped like a cube beside the object shaped like a cone. **2.** Which shape is a hexagon? Color the hexagon. **3.** How many tiles are there? Write the number.

626 six hundred twenty-six

FOR MORE PRACTICE
GO TO THE
Personal Math Trainer

Name _____

In Front Of and Behind

Essential Question How can you use the terms *in front of* and *behind* to describe shapes in the environment?

Common Core Geometry—K.G.A.1

MATHEMATICAL PRACTICES
MP3, MP4, MP6

Listen and Draw *Real World*

DIRECTIONS Trace the X on the object shaped like a sphere that is in front of the object shaped like a cube. Trace the circle around the object shaped like a cylinder that is behind the object shaped like a cube.

Chapter 10 • Lesson 10

six hundred twenty-seven **627**

Share and Show

DIRECTIONS 1. Mark an X on the object shaped like a cylinder that is behind the object shaped like a cube. Draw a circle around the object shaped like a sphere that is directly in front of the object shaped like a cone. Use the words *in front of* and *behind* to name the position of other shapes.

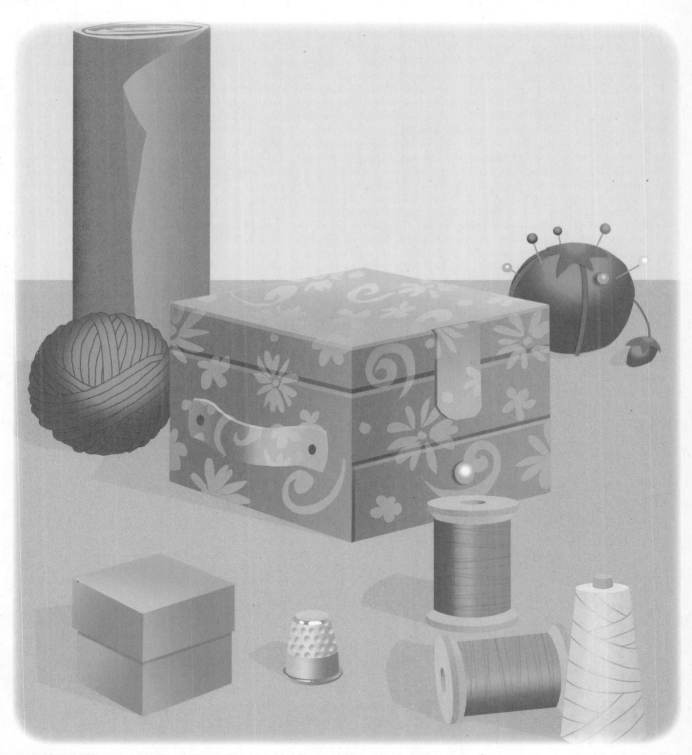

DIRECTIONS **2.** Mark an X on the object shaped like a cube that is in front of the object shaped like a cylinder. Draw a circle around the object shaped like a cylinder that is behind the object shaped like a sphere. Use the words *in front of* and *behind* to name the position of other shaped objects.

Problem Solving • Applications

3

DIRECTIONS **3.** Draw or use pictures to show what you know about real world three-dimensional objects in front of and behind other objects.

 HOME ACTIVITY • Tell your child you are thinking of something in the room that is in front of or behind another object. Have your child tell you the shape of the object.

630 six hundred thirty

In Front Of and Behind

Common Core

COMMON CORE STANDARD—K.G.A.1
Identify and describe shapes (squares, circles, triangles, rectangles, hexagons, cubes, cones, cylinders, and spheres).

DIRECTIONS **I.** Mark an X on the object shaped like a cylinder that is behind the object shaped like a cone. Draw a circle around the object shaped like a cylinder that is in front of the object shaped like a cube. Use the words *in front of* and *behind* to name the position of other shapes.

Lesson Check (K.G.A.1)

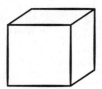 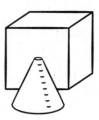

Spiral Review (K.OA.A.1, K.G.A.2)

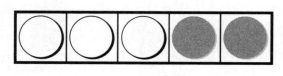

_____ _____

— — — — — — — —

_____ **and** _____

DIRECTIONS I. Circle the set that shows an object shaped like a cone in front of the object shaped like a cube. **2.** Which shape is a triangle? Color the triangle. **3.** How many of each color counter? Write the numbers.

632 six hundred thirty-two

✓ Chapter 10 Review/Test

Personal Math Trainer
Online Assessment
and Intervention

 ①

○　　　　　○　　　　　○　　　　　○

 ②

Personal Math Trainer

③ **THINK SMARTER +**

6 sides　　Yes　　No

curved surface　　Yes　　No

DIRECTIONS 1. Mark under all the shapes that stack. 2. Which objects are shaped like a sphere? Mark an X on each of those objects. 3. Do the words describe a cube? Circle Yes or No.

4

5

6 THINK SMARTER +

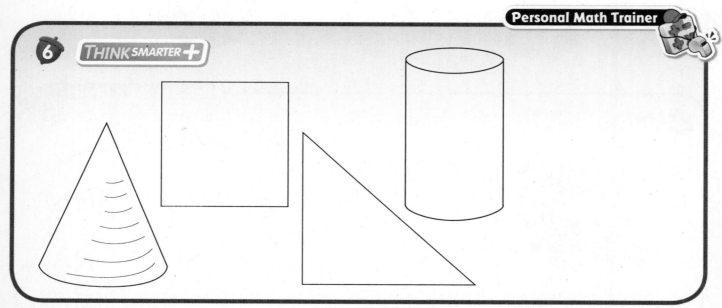

DIRECTIONS **4.** Draw lines to match the objects to their shapes.
5. Which objects are shaped like a cone? Mark an X on each of those
objects. **6.** Color the solid shapes blue. Color the flat shapes red. Draw
another flat shape that is different.

634 six hundred thirty-four

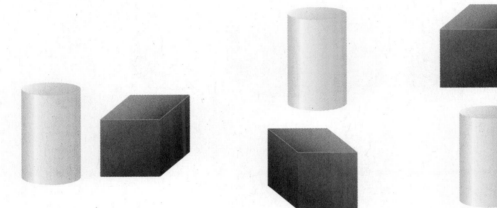

DIRECTIONS **7.** Draw an object that has the shape of a cylinder.
8. Circle the shapes that show the cylinder above the cube.   **9.** Mark an X
on the object shaped like a cylinder next to the object shaped like a cone.

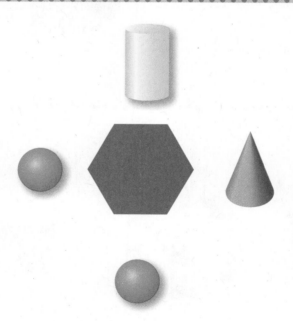

DIRECTIONS **10.** Mark an X on the cone in front of the cube. **11.** Mark an X on the cube that is beside the cone. **12.** Mark an X on the sphere that is below the hexagon.

636 six hundred thirty-six

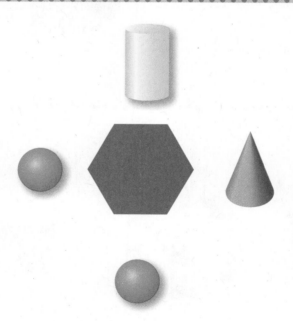

Plants all Around

written by Tami Morton

Common Core **CRITICAL AREA** Representing, relating, and operating on whole numbers, initially with sets of objects

Two leaves fall from a tree.

Circle the leaf that is longer.

Science

Why do plants have leaves?

Two flowers grow near a wall.

Circle the flower that is shorter.

© Houghton Mifflin Harcourt Publishing Company • Image credits: (bn) ©PHOTO 24/Getty Images

Science

Why do plants have flowers?

These carrots grow under the ground.

Circle the carrot that is longer.

Science

Why do plants have roots?

Cattails can be short or tall.

Circle the two cattails that are about the same height.

Science

Why do plants have stems?

One leaf is shorter than the other leaf.

Draw a leaf that is about the same length as the shorter leaf.

Science

How are all these plants the same?

Write About the Story

Draw a purple flower. Make it shorter than the orange flower and taller than the yellow flower.

Vocabulary Review

longer	taller
shorter	same

Longer and Shorter

1. Look at the carrot. Draw a shorter carrot on the left.
Draw a longer carrot on the right.

2. Look at the leaf.
Draw a longer leaf
above it.
Draw a shorter leaf
below it.

Chapter 11 Measurement

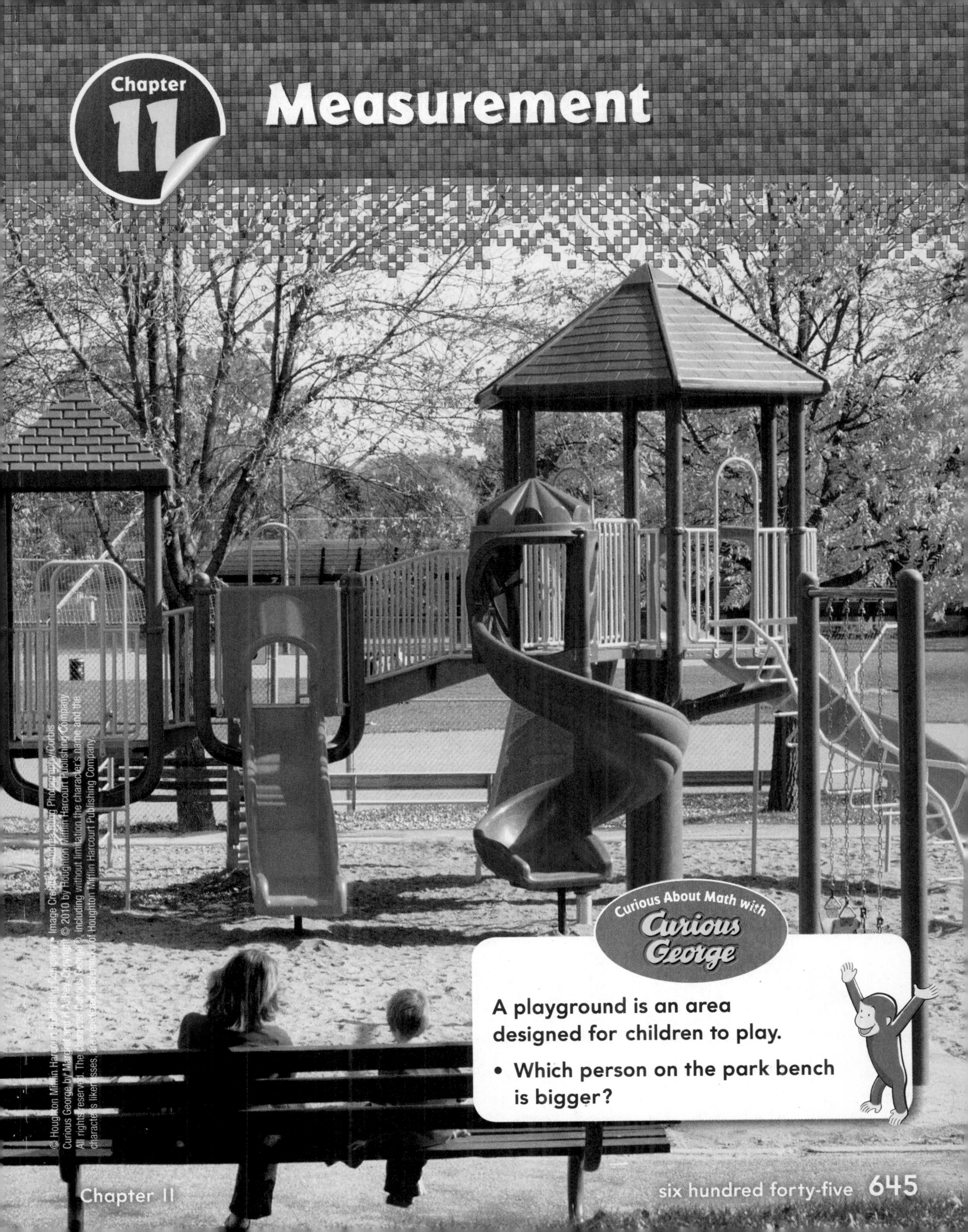
Curious About Math with
Curious George

A playground is an area designed for children to play.

- Which person on the park bench is bigger?

Name _____

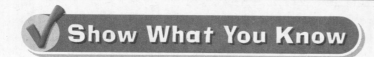
More and Fewer

 1

_____   _____

- - - - - - - - - -   - - - - - - - - - -

_____   _____

 2

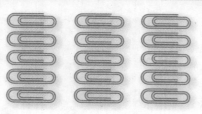   

_____   _____

- - - - - - - - - -   - - - - - - - - - -

Compare Numbers

_____

- - - - - - - - - -

 3

_____

- - - - - - - - - -

_____

This page checks understanding of important skills needed for success in Chapter 11.

DIRECTIONS 1. Write how many in each set. Circle the set with
fewer objects. **2.** Write how many in each set. Circle the set with more
objects. **3.** Write how many cubes in each set. Circle the greater number.

Name _____

Vocabulary Builder

bigger

smaller

DIRECTIONS Are there more flowers in the bigger pot or the smaller pot? Circle to show the pot with more flowers.

• **Interactive Student Edition**
• **Multimedia eGlossary**

Chapter 11

Game
Connecting Cube Challenge

DIRECTIONS Take turns with a partner tossing the number cube. Move your marker that number of spaces. If a player lands on a cube, he or she takes a cube for making a cube train. At the end of the game, players compare cube trains. Each player identifies the number of cubes in his or her cube train. If one player has a greater number of cubes, partners should identify that as the larger quantity of cubes.

MATERIALS game markers, number cube (1–6), connecting cubes

Chapter 11 Vocabulary

heavier

más pesado

33

lighter

más liviano

39

longer

más largo

40

same height

de la misma altura

55

same length

del mismo largo

56

same weight

del mismo peso

58

shorter

más corto

62

taller

más alto

73

lighter

heavier

same height

longer

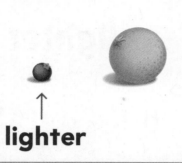

same weight

same length

taller

shorter

Game

Measurement

heavier

lighter

longer

shorter

taller

same height

same length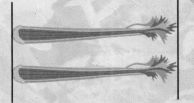

same weight

DIRECTIONS Say each word. Tell something you know about the word.

Game

heavier

same weight

FINISH

shorter

same length

DIRECTIONS Place game pieces on START. Play with a partner. Take turns. Toss the number cube. Move that many spaces. If a player lands on a space with a word or words, he or she uses connecting cubes to model and tell about the word. If the model is correct, the player gets 1 point. When a player has 5 points, follow the closest green path to FINISH. The first player to reach FINISH wins.

MATERIALS 2-color counter game piece for each player, number cube, red and blue connecting cubes

Game

taller

same
height

lighter

FINISH

longer

START ▶

The Write Way

DIRECTIONS Draw to show how to compare the length of two objects.
Reflect Be ready to tell about your drawing.

Name _____

Compare Lengths

Essential Question How can you compare the lengths of two objects?

Common Core **Measurement and Data—K.MD.A.2**

MATHEMATICAL PRACTICES
MP3, MP5, MP6

Listen and Draw *Real World*

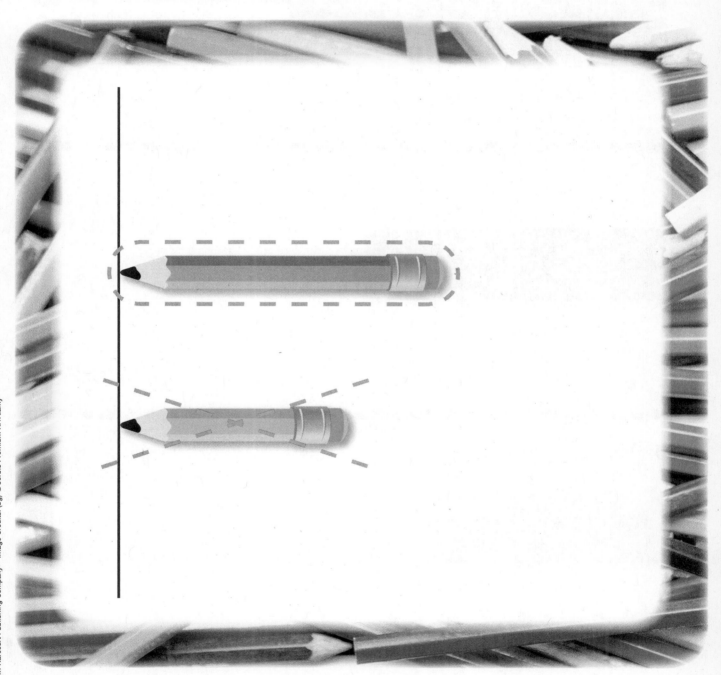

DIRECTIONS Look at the pencils. Compare the lengths of the two pencils. Use the words *longer than*, *shorter than*, or *about the same length* to describe the lengths. Trace the circle around the longer pencil. Trace the X on the shorter pencil.

Chapter 11 • Lesson 1

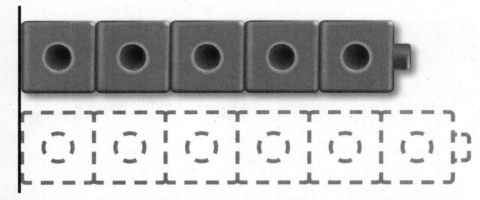

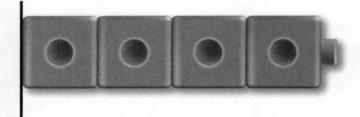

DIRECTIONS **1.** Place cubes on the longer cube train. Trace and color the cube train. **2–3.** Make a cube train that is longer than the cube train shown. Draw and color the cube train.

4 ✓

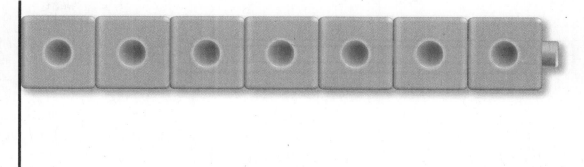

5

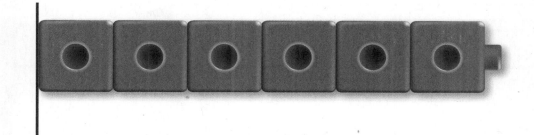

6

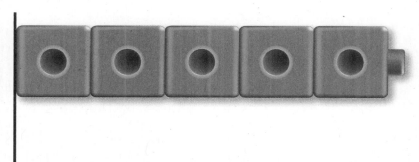

DIRECTIONS 4–6. Make a cube train that is shorter than the cube train shown. Draw and color the cube train.

Problem Solving · Applications

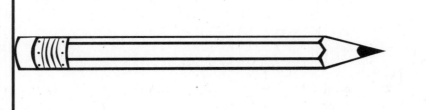

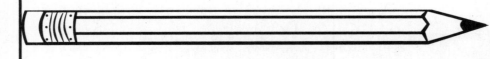

DIRECTIONS **7.** Two of these pencils are about the same length. Color those pencils. **8.** Draw to show what you know about two objects that are about the same length. Tell a friend about your drawing.

 HOME ACTIVITY • Show your child a pencil and ask him or her to find an object that is longer than the pencil. Repeat with an object that is shorter than the pencil.

Compare Lengths

Common Core

COMMON CORE STANDARD—K.MD.A.2
Describe and compare measurable attributes.

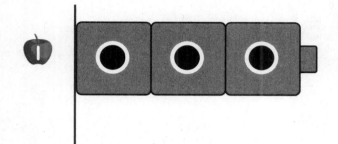

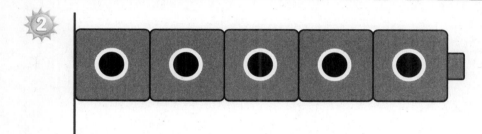

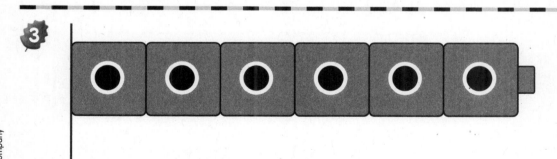

DIRECTIONS **1.** Make a cube train that is longer than the cube train shown. Draw and color the cube train. **2.** Make a cube train that is shorter than the cube train shown. Draw and color the cube train. **3.** Make a cube train that is about the same length as the cube train shown. Draw and color the cube train.

Lesson Check (K.MD.A.2)

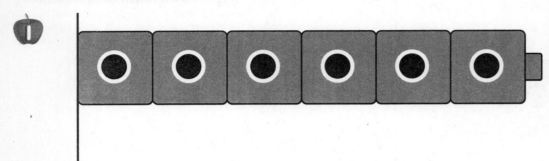

Spiral Review (K.G.A.2, K.G.B.4)

2

3

DIRECTIONS **I.** Make a cube train that is shorter than the cube train shown. Draw and color the cube train. **2.** Which shape is a sphere? Mark an X on the shape. **3.** Look at the shape. Draw a shape that is alike in some way. Tell how the two shapes are alike.

FOR MORE PRACTICE GO TO THE Personal Math Trainer

Name _____

Compare Heights

Essential Question How can you compare
the heights of two objects?

Common Core **Measurement and Data—K.MD.A.2**

MATHEMATICAL PRACTICES
MP3, MP5, MP6

Listen and Draw

DIRECTIONS Look at the chairs. Compare the heights of the two
chairs. Use the words *taller than*, *shorter than*, or *about the same height*
to describe the heights. Trace the circle around the taller chair. Trace
the X on the shorter chair.

Chapter 11 • Lesson 2

six hundred fifty-five **655**

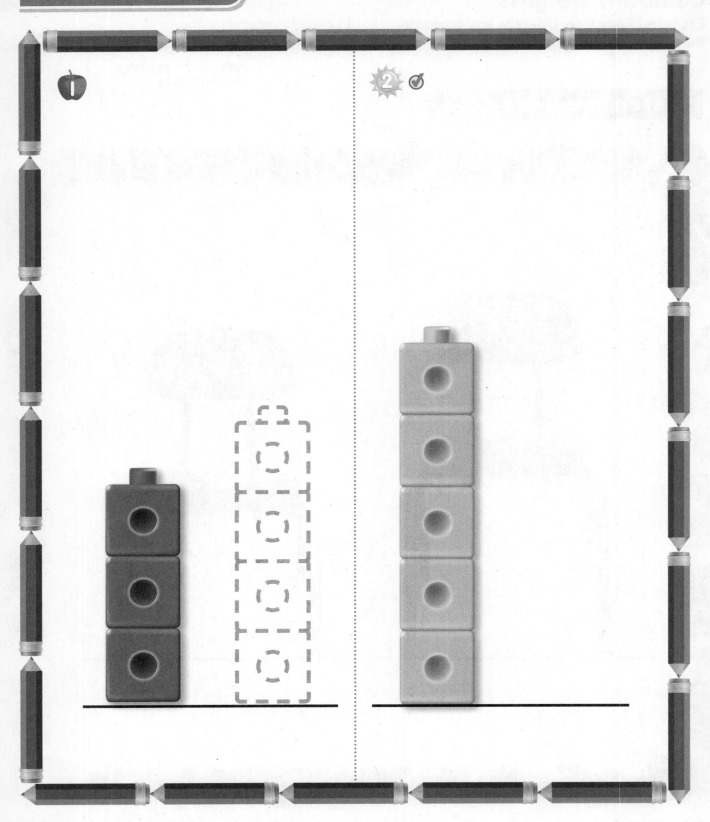

DIRECTIONS 1. Place cubes on the taller cube tower. Trace and color the cube tower. 2. Make a cube tower that is taller than the cube tower shown. Draw and color the cube tower.

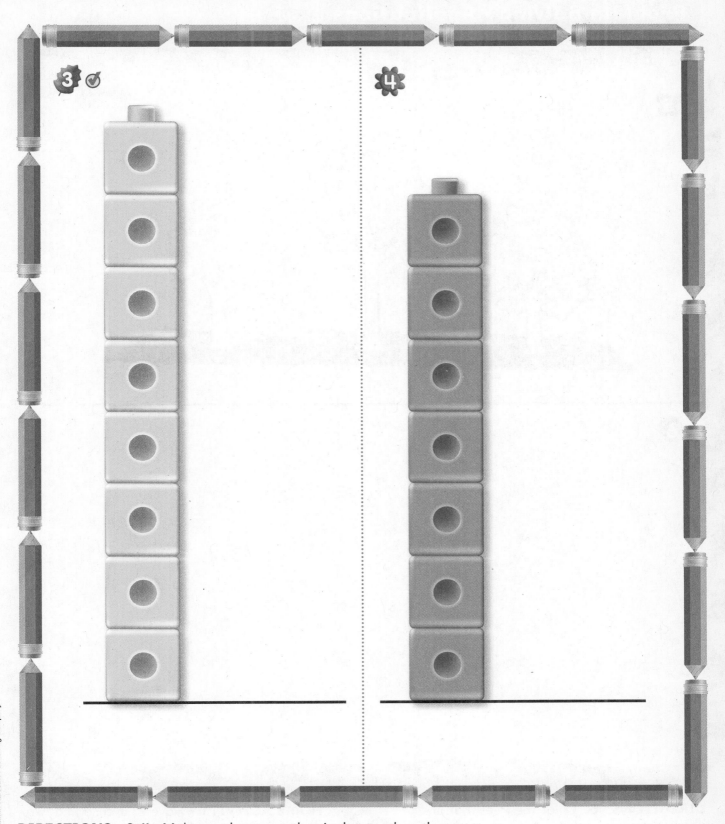

DIRECTIONS 3-4. Make a cube tower that is shorter than the cube tower shown. Draw and color the cube tower.

Problem Solving • Applications

5

6

DIRECTIONS 5. Color the trees that are about the same height.   **6.** Draw to show what you know about two cube towers that are about the same height. Tell a friend about your drawing.

HOME ACTIVITY • Have your child find two objects, such as plastic toys or stuffed animals. Have him or her place the objects side by side to compare the heights. Ask your child which object is taller and which object is shorter.

Compare Heights

Common Core

COMMON CORE STANDARD—K.MD.A.2
Describe and compare measurable attributes.

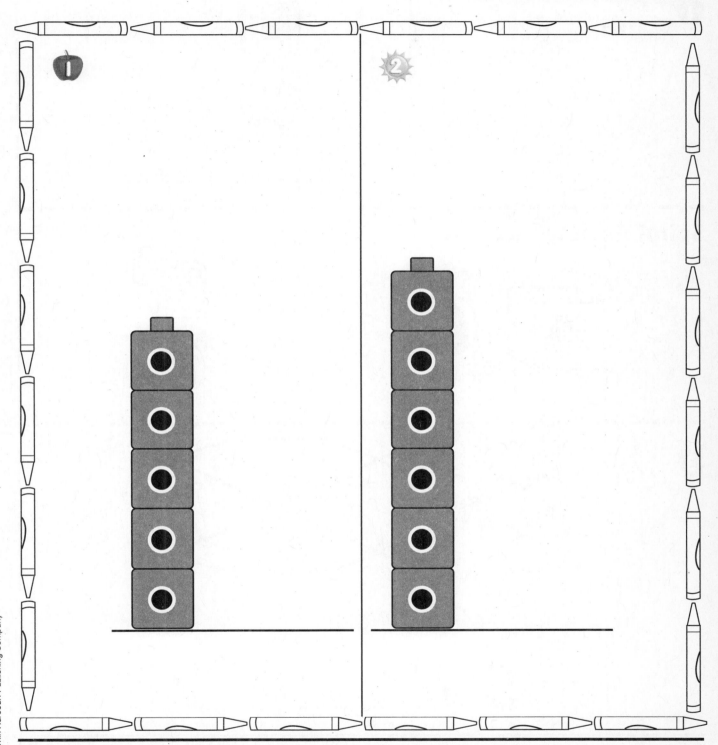

DIRECTIONS **1.** Make a cube tower that is taller than the cube tower shown. Draw and color the cube tower. **2.** Make a cube tower that is shorter than the cube tower shown. Draw and color the cube tower.

Lesson Check (K.MD.A.2)

 1

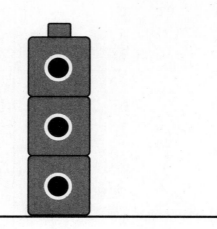

Spiral Review (K.OA.A.5, K.G.A.1)

 2

 3

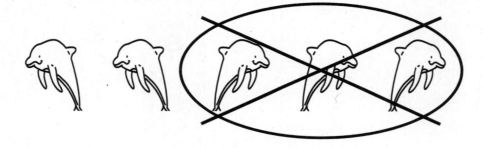

$$5 - \underline{} = 2$$

DIRECTIONS **1.** Make a cube tower that is shorter than the cube
tower shown. Draw and color the cube tower. **2.** Circle the set that
shows an object shaped like a sphere below the object shaped like a
cube. **3.** How many are being taken from the set? Write the number.

660 six hundred sixty

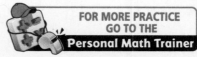
FOR MORE PRACTICE
GO TO THE
Personal Math Trainer

Name _____

Problem Solving • Direct Comparison

Essential Question How can you solve problems using the strategy *draw a picture?*

 Common Core Measurement and Data—K.MD.A.2

MATHEMATICAL PRACTICES
MP1, MP3, MP6

 Unlock the Problem

© Houghton Mifflin Harcourt Publishing Company • Image Credits: ©Bryan Mullennix/Getty Images

DIRECTIONS Compare the lengths or heights of two classroom objects. Draw the objects. Tell a friend about your drawing.

Chapter 11 • Lesson 3

DIRECTIONS 1. Find two small classroom objects. Place one end of each object on the line. Compare the lengths. Draw the objects. Say *longer than*, *shorter than*, or *about the same length* to describe the lengths. Circle both objects if they are about the same length. Circle the longer object if one object is longer than the other.

Name _____

② ✓

DIRECTIONS **2.** Find two small classroom objects. Place one end of each object on the line. Compare the heights. Draw the objects. Say *taller than*, *shorter than*, or *about the same height* to describe the heights. Circle both objects if they are about the same height. Circle the shorter object if one object is shorter than the other.

HOME ACTIVITY • Show your child two objects of different lengths. Have him or her put the ends of the objects on a straight line to compare the lengths and tell which object is shorter and which object is longer.

Personal Math Trainer
Online Assessment
and Intervention

Concepts and Skills

1

2

3

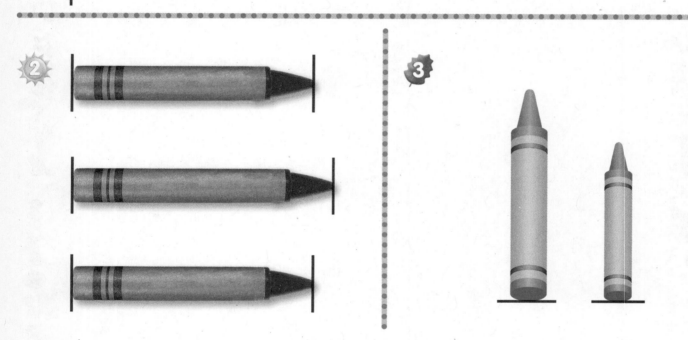

4 THINK SMARTER

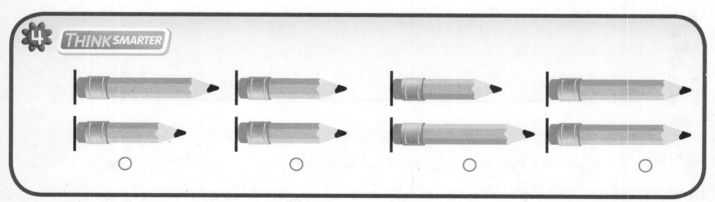

○   ○   ○   ○

DIRECTIONS **1.** Make a cube train that is shorter than the one shown. Draw the cube train. (K.MD.A.2) **2.** Circle the crayons that are about the same length. (K.MD.A.2) **3.** Circle the crayon that is shorter. (.K.MD.A.2) **4.** Choose all the sets with two pencils that are about the same length. (K.MD.A.2)

Name _____

Problem Solving • Direct Comparison

Common Core **COMMON CORE STANDARD—K.MD.A.2**
Describe and compare measurable attributes.

1

- -

2

DIRECTIONS 1. Find two small classroom objects. Place one end of each object on the line. Compare the lengths. Draw the objects. Say *longer than*, *shorter than*, or *about the same length* to describe the lengths. Circle both objects if they are about the same length. Circle the longer object if one object is longer than the other. **2.** Find two small classroom objects. Place one end of each object on the line. Compare the heights. Draw the objects. Say *taller than*, *shorter than*, or *about the same height* to describe the heights. Circle both objects if they are about the same height. Circle the shorter object if one object is shorter than the other.

Chapter 11

Lesson Check (K.MD.A.2)

Spiral Review (K.OA.A.2, K.G.B.4)

 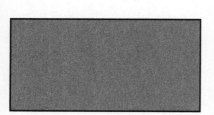

_____ vertices

 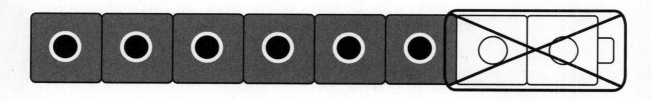

DIRECTIONS 1. Find two pencils. Place one end of each pencil on the line. Compare the lengths. Draw the pencils. Say *longer than*, *shorter than*, or *about the same length* to describe the lengths. Circle both pencils if they are about the same length. Circle the shorter pencil if one pencil is shorter than the other. 2. How many vertices does the rectangle have? Write the number. 3. Use the cubes to complete the subtraction sentence.

FOR MORE PRACTICE GO TO THE Personal Math Trainer

Name _____

Compare Weights

Essential Question How can you compare the weights of two objects?

Common Core **Measurement and Data—K.MD.A.2**

MATHEMATICAL PRACTICES
MP3, MP5, MP6

Listen and Draw *Real World*

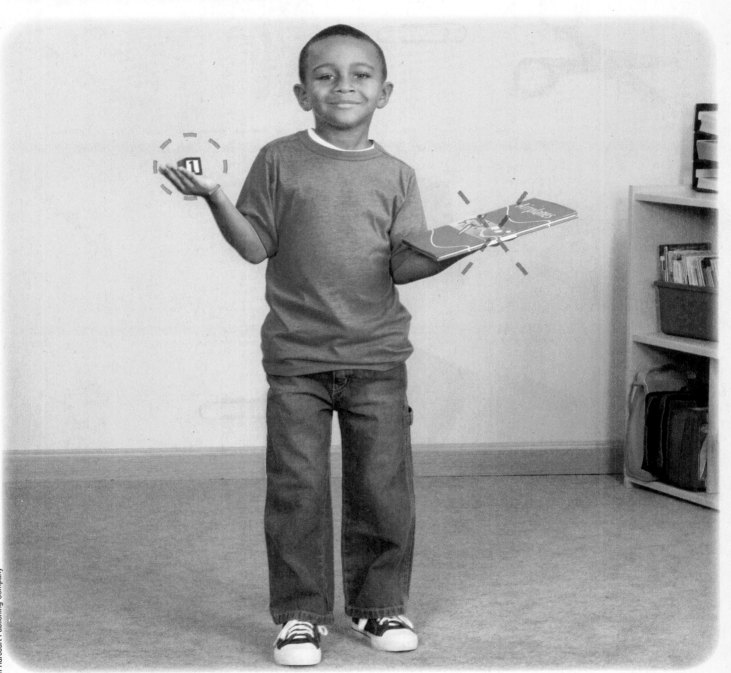

DIRECTIONS Look at the picture. Compare the weights of the two objects. Use the words *heavier than*, *lighter than*, or *about the same weight* to describe the weights. Trace the circle around the lighter object. Trace the X on the heavier object.

Chapter 11 • Lesson 4

 left  right

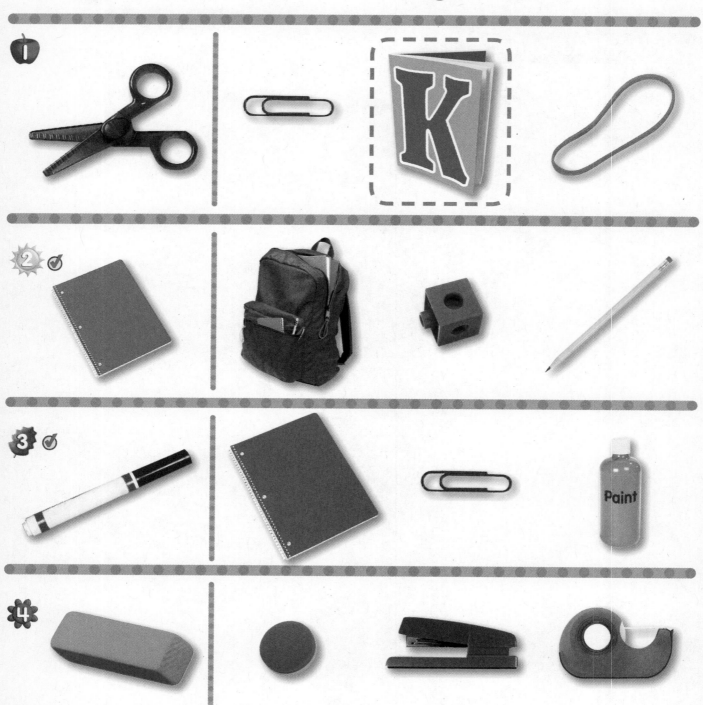

DIRECTIONS Find the first object in the row, and hold it in your left hand. Find the rest of the objects in the row, and take turns holding each of the objects in your right hand. **1.** Trace to show the object that is heavier than the object in your left hand. **2.** Circle the object that is heavier than the object in your left hand. **3–4.** Circle the object that is lighter than the object in your left hand.

5

6

DIRECTIONS Find a book in the classroom. **5.** Find a classroom object that is lighter than the book. Draw it in the work space. **6.** Find a classroom object that is heavier than the book. Draw it in the work space.

Problem Solving • Applications Real World

7

WRITE Math

DIRECTIONS 7. Draw to show what you know about comparing the weights of two objects. Tell a friend about your drawing.

HOME ACTIVITY • Have your child compare the weights of two objects in a house. Then have him or her use the terms *heavier* and *lighter* to describe the weights.

Compare Weights

Common Core **COMMON CORE STANDARD—K.MD.A.2**
Describe and compare measurable attributes.

 left   right

1

2

3

4

DIRECTIONS Find the first object in the row, and hold it in your left hand. Find the rest of the objects in the row, and hold each object in your right hand. **1–2.** Circle the object that is lighter than the object in your left hand. **3–4.** Circle the object that is heavier than the object in your left hand.

Lesson Check (K.MD.A.2)

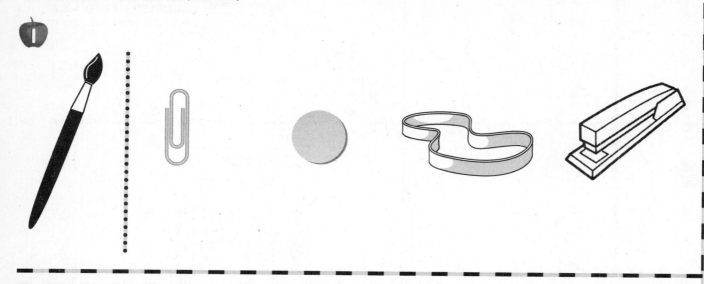

Spiral Review (K.CC.C.6, K.G.A.3)

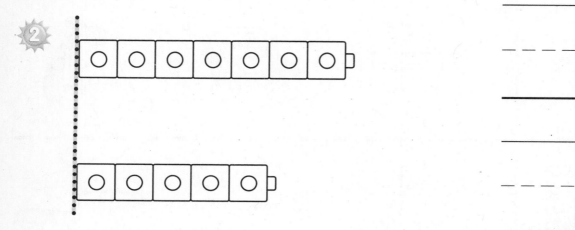

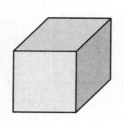 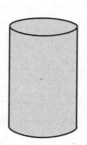 

DIRECTIONS **1.** Find a paintbrush. Hold it in your left hand. Find the rest of the objects in the row, and hold each object in your right hand. Circle the object that is heavier than the paintbrush. **2.** Count the cubes. Write how many. Circle the number that is less. **3.** Which is a two-dimensional or flat shape? Mark an X on the shape.

FOR MORE PRACTICE GO TO THE Personal Math Trainer

Name _____

Length, Height, and Weight

Essential Question How can you describe several ways to measure one object?

Common Core Measurement and Data—K.MD.A.1

MATHEMATICAL PRACTICES
MP1, MP3, MP6

Listen and Draw Real World

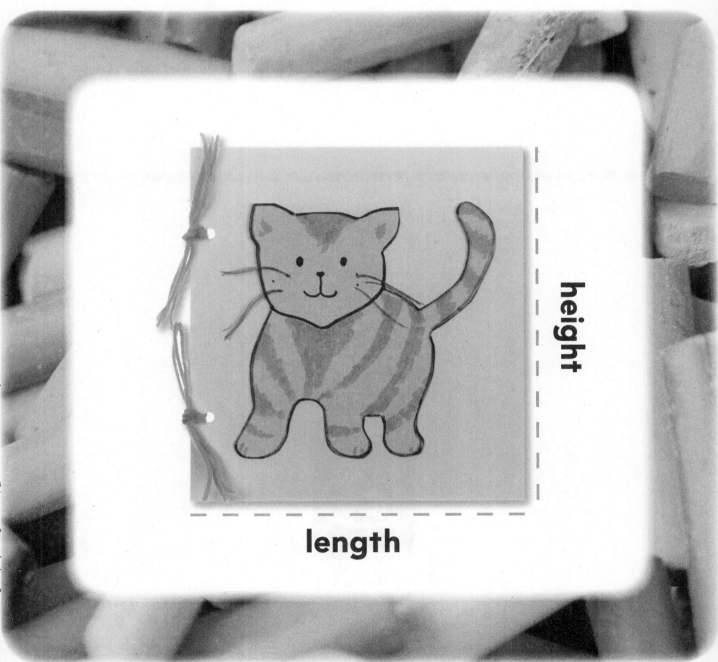

height

length

DIRECTIONS Look at the book. Trace your finger over the line that shows how to measure the height of the book. Trace your finger over the line that shows how to measure the length of the book. Talk about another way to measure the book.

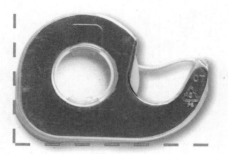

DIRECTIONS 1–2. Use red to trace the line that shows how to measure the length. Use blue to trace the line that shows how to measure the height. Talk about another way to measure the object.

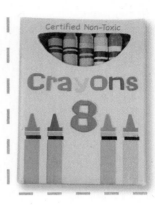

DIRECTIONS 3–6. Use red to trace the line that shows how to measure the length. Use blue to trace the line that shows how to measure the height. Talk about another way to measure the object.

Problem Solving • Applications

DIRECTIONS 7. Draw to show what you know about measuring an object in more than one way.

HOME ACTIVITY • Show your child an object in the house that can be easily measured by length, height, and weight. Ask him or her to describe the different ways to measure the object.

Length, Height, and Weight

COMMON CORE STANDARD—K.MD.A.1
Describe and compare measurable attributes.

MATH

Markers

GLUE

DIRECTIONS 1–4. Use red to trace the line that shows how to measure the length. Use blue to trace the line that shows how to measure the height. Talk about another way to measure the object.

Chapter 11

Lesson Check

 1

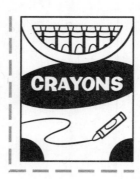

Spiral Review (K.NBT.A.1, K.G.A.2)

 2

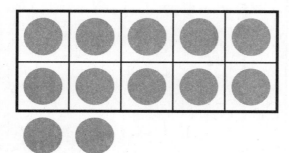

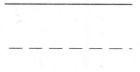

. . . .

3

 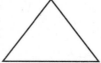

DIRECTIONS 1. Use red to trace the line that shows how to measure the length. Use blue to trace the line that shows how to measure the height. **2.** Count and tell how many. Write the number. **3.** Which shape is a rectangle? Color the rectangle.

**FOR MORE PRACTICE
GO TO THE
Personal Math Trainer**

✓ Chapter 11 Review/Test

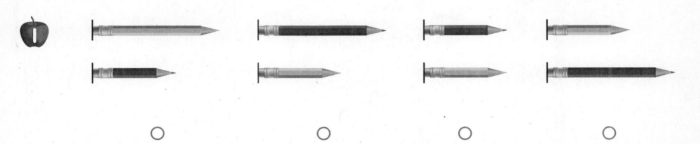

○   ○   ○   ○

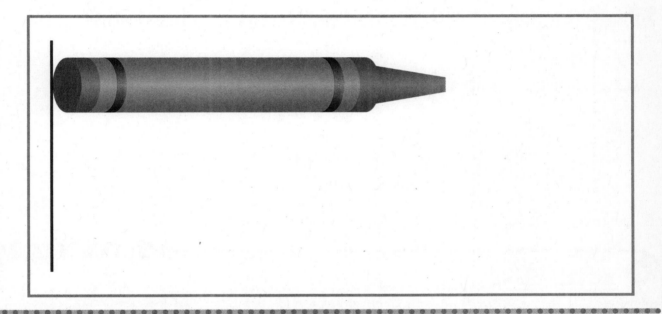

DIRECTIONS **1.** Choose all the sets that have a green pencil that is longer than the orange pencil. **2.** Draw a crayon that is shorter. **3.** Circle the tree that is taller.

Chapter 11

GO DIGITAL Assessment Options
Chapter Test

4

- -

5

Personal Math Trainer

6 THINK SMARTER +

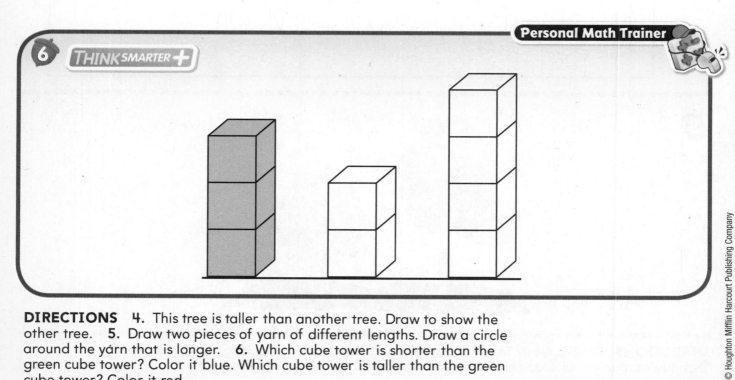

DIRECTIONS **4.** This tree is taller than another tree. Draw to show the other tree. **5.** Draw two pieces of yarn of different lengths. Draw a circle around the yarn that is longer. **6.** Which cube tower is shorter than the green cube tower? Color it blue. Which cube tower is taller than the green cube tower? Color it red.

680 six hundred eighty

Name _____

7

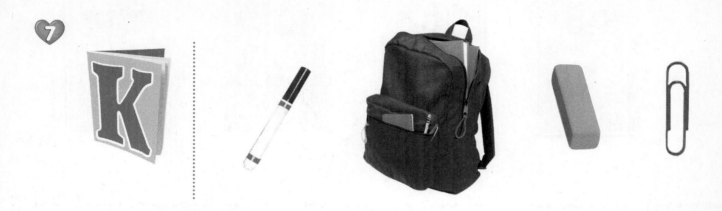

8

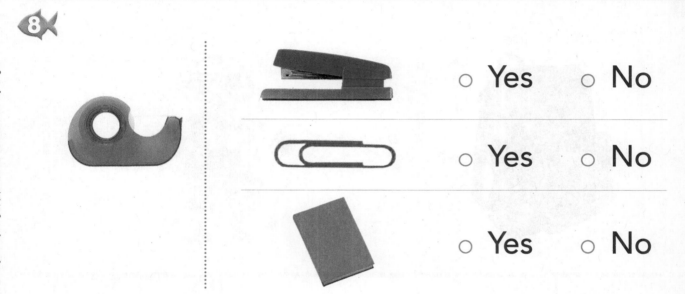

○ Yes   ○ No

○ Yes   ○ No

○ Yes   ○ No

Personal Math Trainer

9 THINK SMARTER ✚

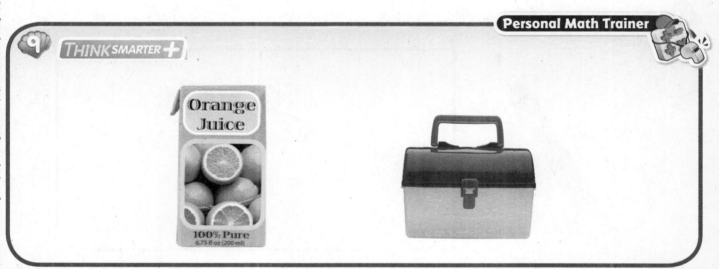

DIRECTIONS **7.** Circle all the objects that are lighter than the book.   **8.** Is the object heavier than the tape dispenser? Choose Yes or No.   **9.** Draw a line to show the height of the juice box. Draw a line to show the length of the lunchbox.

○   ○   ○   ○

   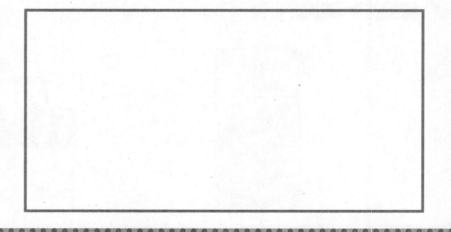

DIRECTIONS 10. Choose all of the pictures that have lines that show how to measure height. 11. Look at the objects. Mark an X on the lighter object. Circle the heavier object. 12. Draw an object that is heavier than the pencil.

© Houghton Mifflin Harcourt Publishing Company • Image Credits: (cl) ©Siede Preis/PhotoDisc/Getty Images; (cr) ©Stockbyte/Getty Images

Classify and Sort Data

Curious About Math with
Curious George

Primary colors are blue, red, and yellow.

- How many primary colors is the girl sorting?

Name _____

Color and Shape

1

2

Compare Sets

3
   _____

   _____

4
   _____

   _____

This page checks understanding of important skills needed for success in Chapter 12.

DIRECTIONS 1. Circle the fruits that are red. 2. Circle the triangles. 3. Count and write how many in each set. Circle the set with more objects. 4. Count and write how many in each set. Circle the set with fewer objects.

Vocabulary Builder

different

alike

DIRECTIONS Tell what you know about the ladybugs. Some of the ladybugs are different. Circle those ladybugs and tell why they are different. Tell what you know about the butterflies.

- **Interactive Student Edition**
- **Multimedia *eGlossary***

Chapter 12

Chapter 12 **Game** **At the Farm**

DIRECTIONS Use the picture to play with a partner. Decide who will go first. Player 1 looks at the picture, selects an object, and tells Player 2 the color of the object. Player 2 must guess what Player 1 sees. Once Player 2 guesses correctly, it is his or her turn to choose an object and have Player 1 guess.

Chapter 12 Vocabulary

big

grande

8

color (blue)

color (azul)

9

category

categoría

10

classify

clasificar

12

graph

gráfica

30

color (green)

color (verde)

32

color (red)

color (rojo)

53

shape

forma

61

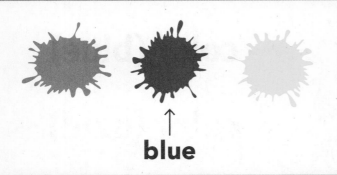

blue

big

apples

not apples

classify

fruits

toys

category

green

Sorting Animals

graph

shape

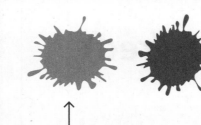

red

Chapter 12 Vocabulary *(continued)*

size tamaño 66	**small** pequeño 68
color (yellow) color (amarillo) 85	**zero** cero, ninguno 86

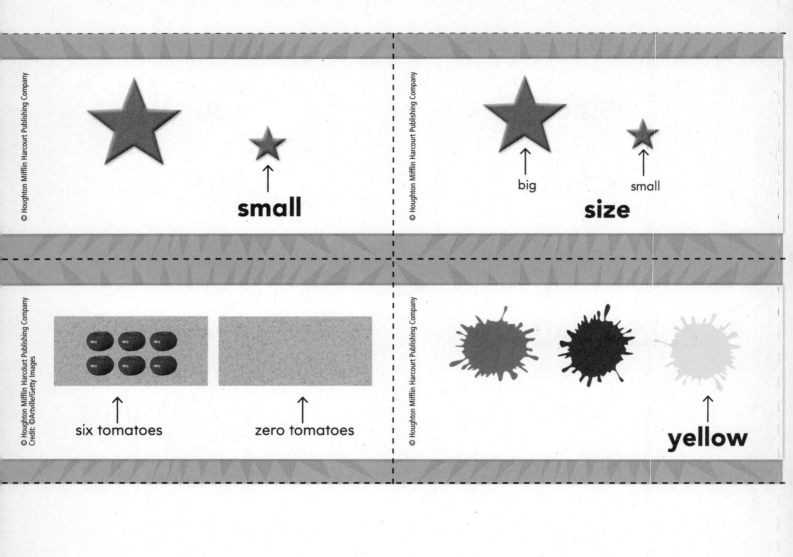

small

big   small

size

six tomatoes   zero tomatoes

yellow

Guess the Word

Word Box

red
blue
green
yellow
classify
category
shape
size
small
big
graph

Secret Words

Player 1

Player 2

DIRECTIONS Players take turns. A player chooses a secret word from the Word Box and then sets the timer. The player gives hints about the secret word. If the other player guesses the secret word before time runs out, he or she puts a connecting cube in the chart. The first player who has connecting cubes in all his or her boxes is the winner.

MATERIALS timer, connecting cubes for each player

The Write Way

© Houghton Mifflin Harcourt Publishing Company • Image Credits: (bg) ©PhotoDisc/Getty Images; (r) ©Debra Hughes/Shutterstock

DIRECTIONS Choose one idea. • Draw to show how to classify objects by size.
• Draw to show a graph. **Reflect** Be ready to tell about your drawing.

Name _____

Algebra • Classify and Count by Color

Essential Question How can you classify and count objects by color?

Common Core Measurement and Data—
K.MD.B.3

MATHEMATICAL PRACTICES
MP2, MP5, MP6

Listen and Draw

   not

DIRECTIONS Choose a color. Use that color crayon to color the clouds. Sort and classify a handful of shapes into a set of that color and a set of not that color. Draw and color the shapes.

❶ ✓

red	**blue**
yellow	**green**

DIRECTIONS I. Place shapes as shown. Sort and classify the shapes by the category of color. Draw and color the shapes in each category.

2

1

| red | blue |
| yellow | green |

_____
- - - - - - -
_____

3

2

| red | blue |
| yellow | green |

_____
- - - - - - -
_____

4

3

| red | blue |
| yellow | green |

_____
- - - - - - -
_____

DIRECTIONS Look at the categories of color in Exercise I. Count how many in each category. **2.** Circle the categories of color that have one shape. Write the number. **3.** Circle the category that has two shapes. Write the number. **4.** Circle the category that has three shapes. Write the number.

Problem Solving • Applications

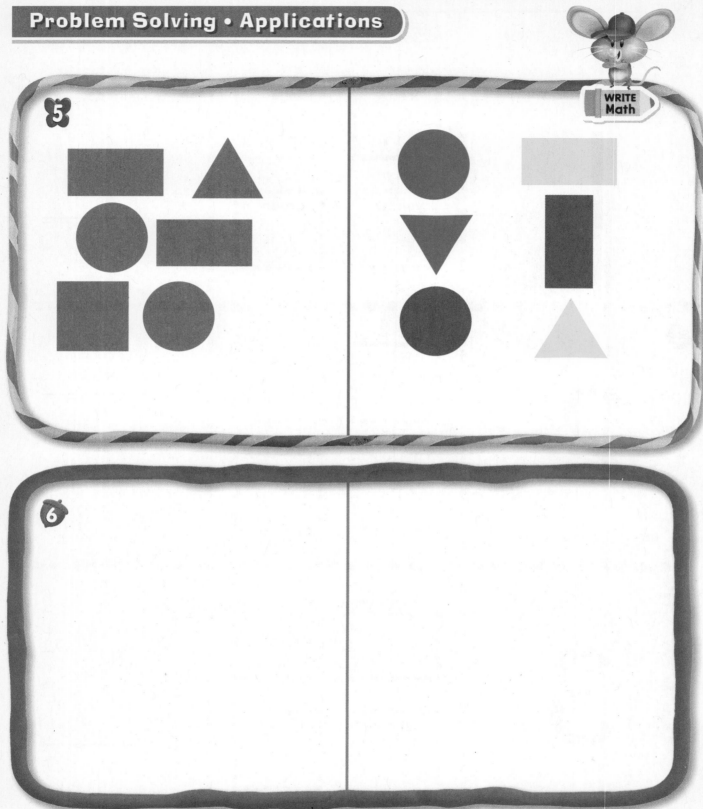

WRITE Math

5

6

DIRECTIONS 5. Ava placed her shapes as shown. How did she sort and classify her shapes? Draw one more shape in each category.   **6.** Draw to show what you know about sorting and classifying by color.

HOME ACTIVITY • Provide your child with different colors of the same objects, such as straws, socks, or toys. Ask him or her to sort and classify the objects into two sets, a set of all one color and a set of all the other colors.

690 six hundred ninety

Algebra • Classify and Count by Color

COMMON CORE STANDARD—K.MD.B.3
Classify objects and count the number of objects in each category.

1

yellow	red

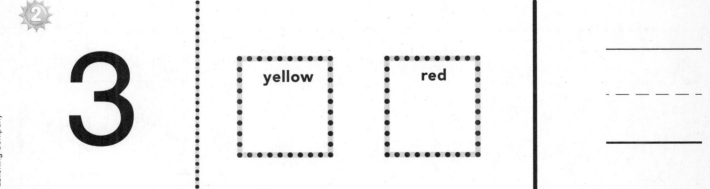

2

3

| yellow | red |

DIRECTIONS   1. Place a yellow square, red triangle, red rectangle, yellow square, and red triangle at the top of the page as shown. Sort and classify the shapes by the category of color. Draw and color the shapes in each category.   **2.** Look at the categories in Exercise 1. Count how many in each category. Circle the category that has 3 shapes. Write the number.

Lesson Check (K.MD.B.3)

Spiral Review (K.CC.A.3, K.G.B.4)

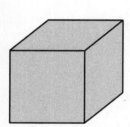 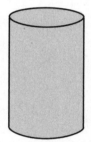 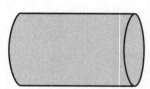

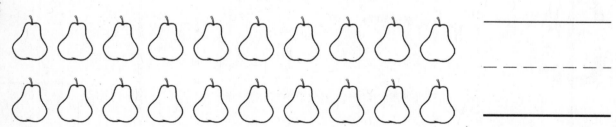

DIRECTIONS 1. Look at the set of shapes. Which shape belongs in the same category? Draw that shape in the box and color it. How many shapes are in the category now? Write the number. **2.** Which shape does not stack? Mark an X on the shape. **3.** Count and tell how many pieces of fruit. Write the number.

FOR MORE PRACTICE
GO TO THE
Personal Math Trainer

Name _____

Algebra • Classify and Count by Shape

Essential Question How can you classify and count objects by shape?

Common Core **Measurement and Data—
K.MD.B.3**

MATHEMATICAL PRACTICES
MP2, MP5, MP6

Listen and Draw

not

DIRECTIONS Choose a shape. Draw the shape at the top of each side. Sort and classify a handful of shapes into a set of the shape you chose and a set that is not that shape. Draw and color the shapes.

Share and Show

1

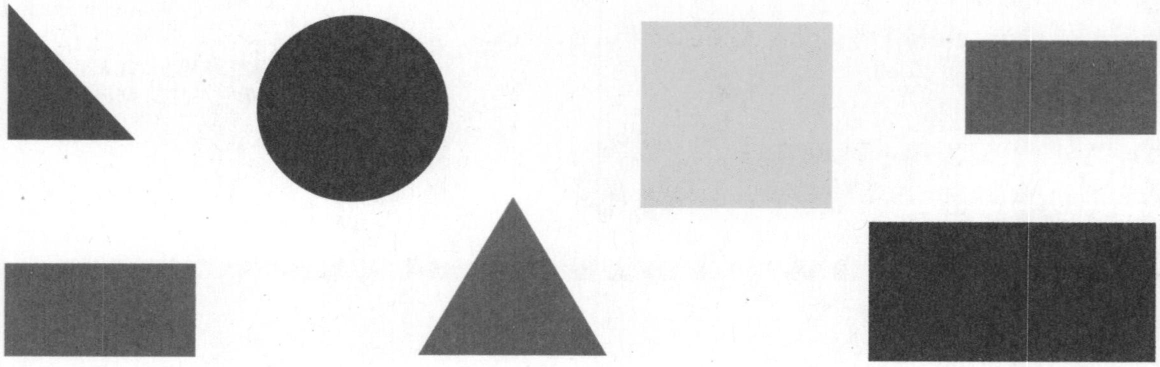

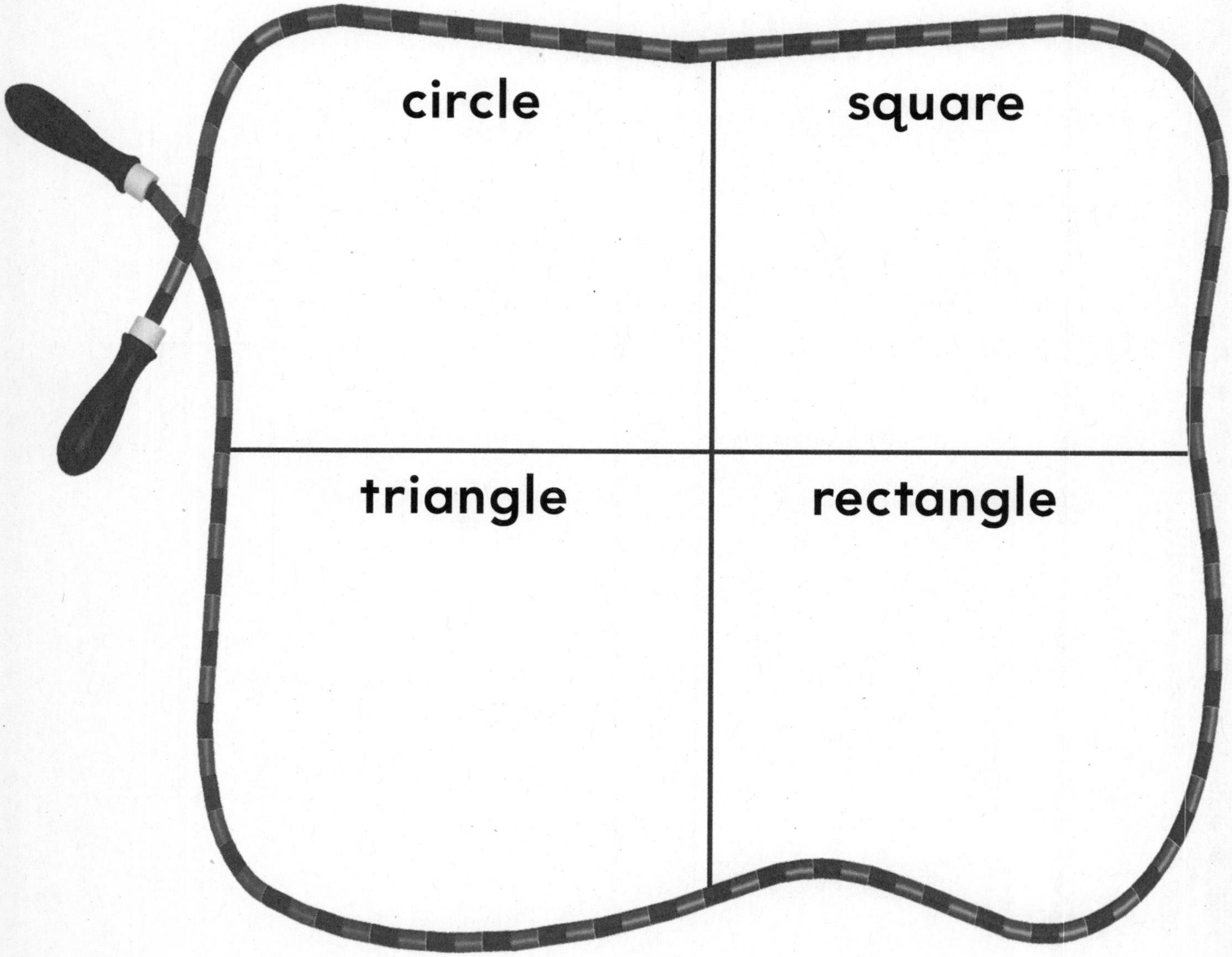
circle
square
triangle
rectangle

DIRECTIONS 1. Place shapes as shown. Sort and classify the shapes by the category of shape. Draw and color the shapes in each category.

Name _____

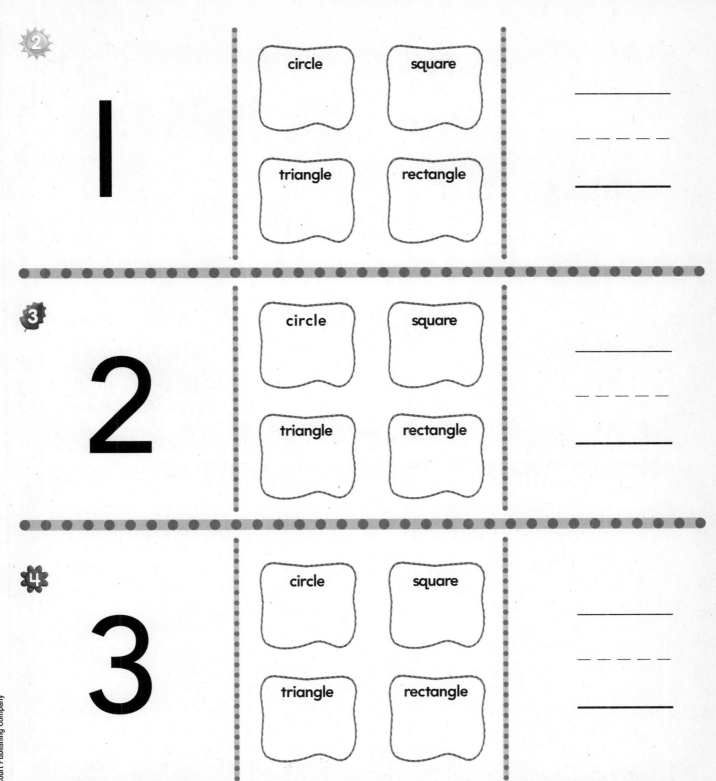

DIRECTIONS Look at the categories of shapes in Exercise 1. Count how many in each category. **2.** Circle the categories of shapes that have one shape. Write the number. **3.** Circle the category that has two shapes. Write the number. **4.** Circle the category that has three shapes. Write the number.

Problem Solving • Applications

DIRECTIONS **5.** Brandon used his shapes. How did he sort and classify his shapes? Draw one more shape in each category. **6.** Using the same shapes, draw to show what you know about sorting and classifying by shape in a different way.

HOME ACTIVITY • Have your child sort objects in a house into categories of shape.

696 six hundred ninety-six

Algebra • Classify and Count by Shape

Common Core **COMMON CORE STANDARD—K.MD.B,3**
Classify objects and count the number of objects in each category.

①

triangle	circle

- -

②

2

triangle	circle

_____

- - - - - - - -

_____

DIRECTIONS 1. Place a green triangle, blue circle, red triangle, and blue circle at the top of the page as shown. Sort and classify the shapes by the category of shape. Draw and color the shapes in each category. 2. Look at the categories in Exercise 1. Count how many in each category. Circle the categories that have two shapes. Write the number.

Lesson Check (K.MD.B.3)

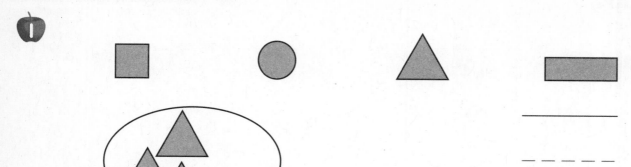

Spiral Review (K.OA.A.3, K.MD.A.2)

②

③

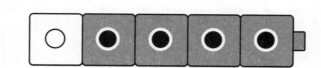

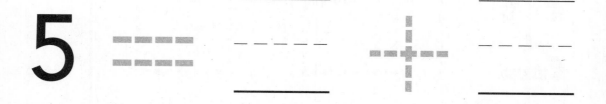

DIRECTIONS **1.** Look at the set of shapes. Which shape belongs in the same category? Draw that shape in the oval. How many shapes are in the category now? Write the number. **2.** Find two crayons. Place one end of each crayon on the line. Compare the lengths. Draw the crayons. Say *longer than*, *shorter than*, or *about the same length* to describe the lengths. Circle both crayons if they are about the same length. Circle the longer crayon if one crayon is longer than the other. **3.** Complete the addition sentence to show the numbers that match the cube train.

698 six hundred ninety-eight

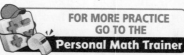

FOR MORE PRACTICE
GO TO THE
Personal Math Trainer

Name _____

Algebra • Classify and Count by Size

Essential Question How can you classify and count objects by size?

Common Core **Measurement and Data—K.MD.B.3**
MATHEMATICAL PRACTICES
MP2, MP5, MP6

Listen and Draw   Hands On

big	small

DIRECTIONS Sort and classify a handful of shapes by size. Draw and color the shapes.

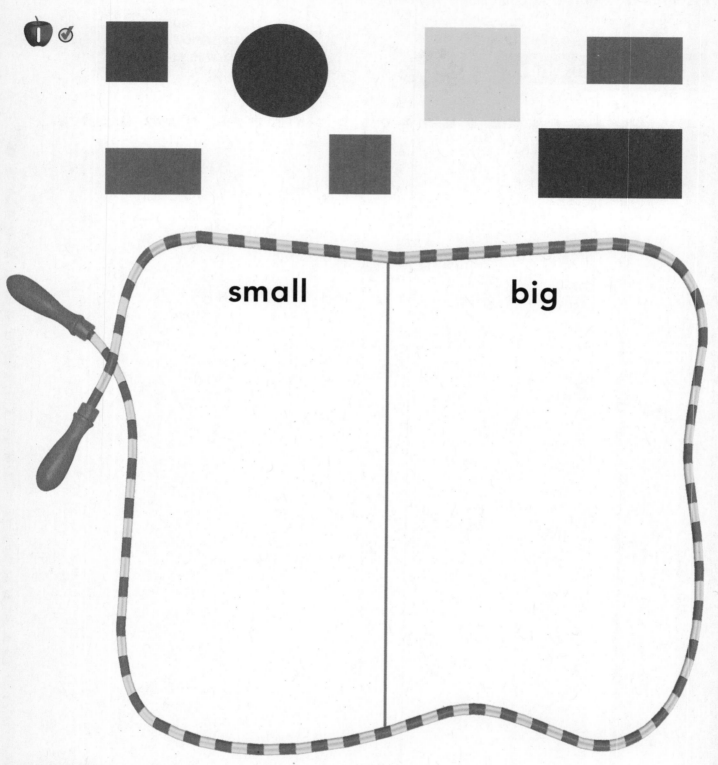

small   big

DIRECTIONS **1.** Place shapes as shown. Sort and classify the shapes by the category of size. Draw and color the shapes in each category.

Name _____

4

small   big

_____
\- \- \- \- \-
_____

3

small   big

_____
\- \- \- \- \-
_____

DIRECTIONS Look at the categories of size in Exercise I. Count how many in each category.
2. Circle the category that has four per category. Write the number. **3.** Circle the category that has three per category. Write the number.

HOME ACTIVITY • Have your child sort objects in a house into categories of size.

© Houghton Mifflin Harcourt Publishing Company

Chapter 12 • Lesson 3

Personal Math Trainer
Online Assessment
and Intervention

Concepts and Skills

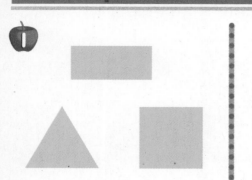

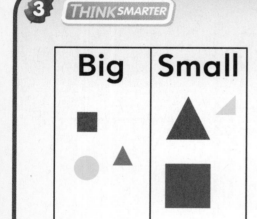
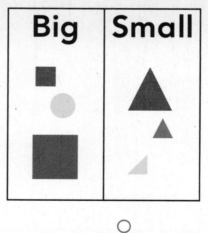
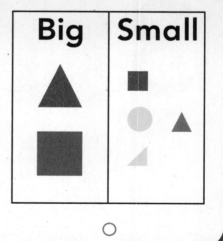

Big	Small	Big	Small	Big	Small

○   ○   ○

DIRECTIONS 1. Look at the set at the beginning of the row. Circle the shape that belongs in that set. (K.MD.B.3) 2. Look at the shape at the beginning of the row. Mark an X on the set in which the shape belongs. (K.MD.B.3) 3. Mark under the chart that shows the shapes correctly classified. (K.MD.B.3)

Algebra • Classify and Count by Size

COMMON CORE STANDARD—K.MD.B.3
Classify objects and count the number of objects in each category.

small	big

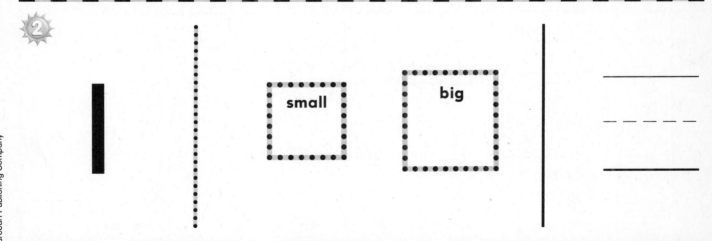

DIRECTIONS 1. Place a yellow square, blue circle, red rectangle, and blue rectangle at the top of the page as shown. Sort and classify the shapes by the category of size. Draw and color the shapes in each category. 2. Look at the categories in Exercise 1. Count how many in each category. Circle the category that has one per category. Write the number.

Lesson Check (K.MD.B.3)

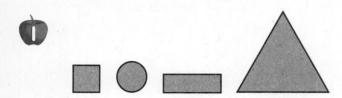

small	big

Spiral Review (K.OA.A.5, K.G.A.2)

_____

- - - - - - - - -

_____

DIRECTIONS **1.** Sort and classify the shapes by the category of size. Draw the shapes in each category. **2.** How many flat surfaces does the cylinder have? Write the number. **3.** Sarah makes a five-cube train. She takes the cube train apart to show how many cubes are gray. Trace and write to show the subtraction sentence for Sarah's cube train.

704 seven hundred four

FOR MORE PRACTICE
GO TO THE
Personal Math Trainer

Name _____

Make a Concrete Graph

Essential Question How can you make a graph to count objects that have been classified into categories?

Common Core Measurement and Data—K.MD.B.3
Also K.CC.C.6
MATHEMATICAL PRACTICES
MP2, MP6, MP8

Listen and Draw

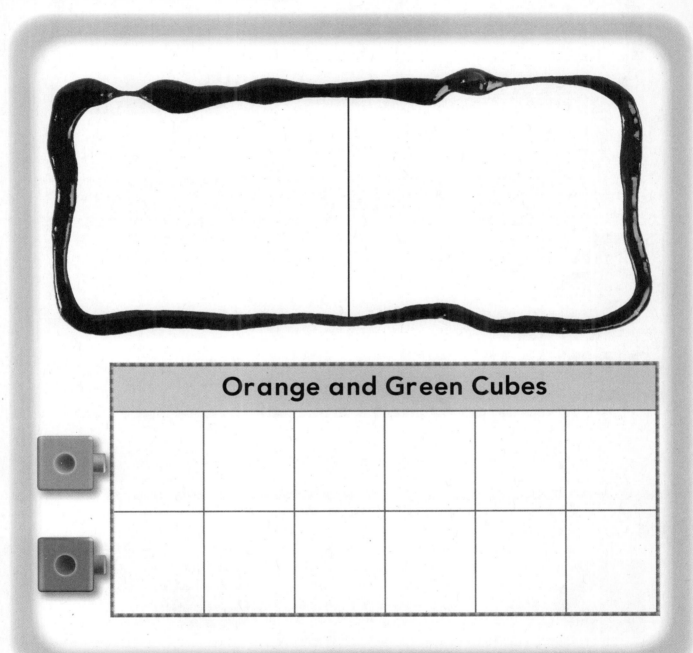

Orange and Green Cubes

DIRECTIONS Place a handful of orange and green cubes on the workspace. Sort and classify the cubes by the category of color. Move the cubes to the graph by category. Draw and color the cubes. Tell a friend how many in each category.

1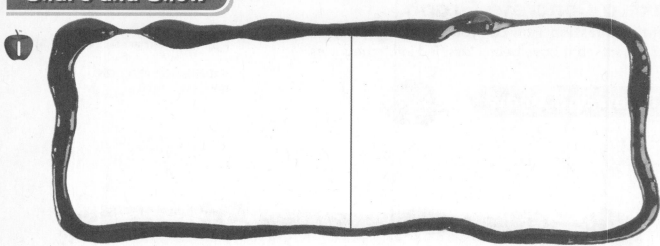

2 ☑

Red and Blue Cubes				

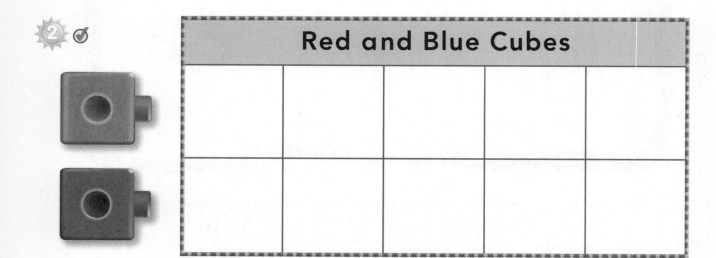

3 ☑

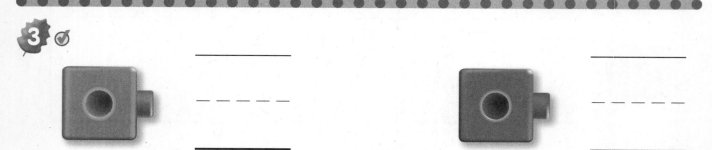

DIRECTIONS **1.** Place a handful of red and blue cubes on the workspace. Sort and classify the cubes by category. **2.** Move the cubes to the graph. Draw and color the cubes. **3.** Write how many of each cube.

706 seven hundred six

4

5

Green Circles and Triangles

6

_____   _____

- - - - - - -   - - - - - - -

_____   _____

DIRECTIONS **4.** Place a handful of green circles and triangles on the workspace. Sort and classify the shapes by category. **5.** Move the shapes to the graph. Draw and color the shapes. **6.** Write how many of each shape.

Problem Solving • Applications

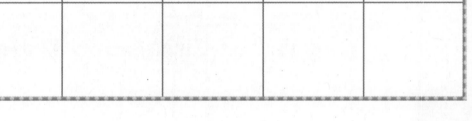

My Graph

 _____

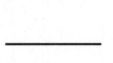 _____

 _____

_____

DIRECTIONS 7. Use five cubes of two colors. Color the cubes to show the categories. Draw and color to show what you know about making a graph with those cubes. How many are in each category? Write the numbers.

HOME ACTIVITY • Have your child tell about the graph that he or she made on this page.

Make a Concrete Graph

Common Core

COMMON CORE STANDARD—K.MD.B.3
Classify objects and count the number of objects in each category.

1

2

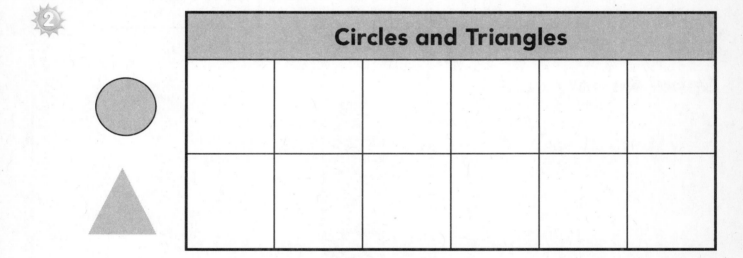

Circles and Triangles					

3

DIRECTIONS **1.** Place a handful of green circles and triangles on the workspace. Sort and classify the shapes by category. **2.** Move the shapes to the graph. Draw and color the shapes. **3.** Write how many of each shape.

Triangles and Squares				

_____   _____

- - - - - - - - - - -   - - - - - - - - - - -

_____   _____

Spiral Review (K.CC.A.3, K.MD.A.2)

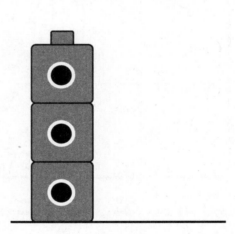

_____

- - - - - - - - - - -

_____

DIRECTIONS 1. Look at the shapes. Draw and color the shapes in the graph. Write how many of each shape. 2. Make a cube train that is about the same height as the cube train shown. Draw and color the cube train. 3. How many tiles are there? Write the number.

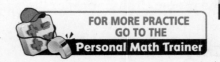

FOR MORE PRACTICE
GO TO THE
Personal Math Trainer

Name _____

Problem Solving • Read a Graph

Essential Question How can you read a graph to count objects that have been classified into categories?

Common Core — **Measurement and Data—K.MD.B.3**
Also K.CC.C.6
MATHEMATICAL PRACTICES
MP2, MP6, MP8

Unlock the Problem

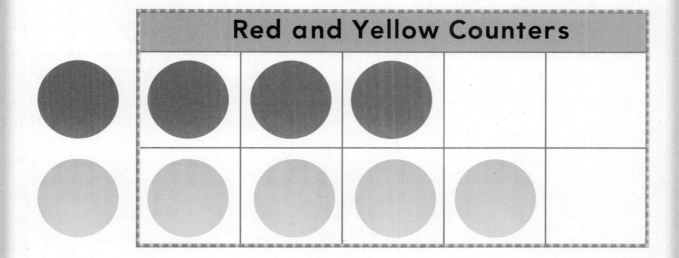

Red and Yellow Counters

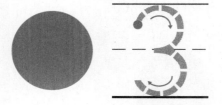

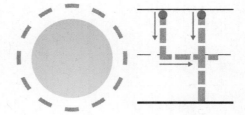

DIRECTIONS Erin made a graph of her counters. How many counters are in each category? Trace the numbers. Trace the circle to show which category has more counters.

Chapter 12 • Lesson 5

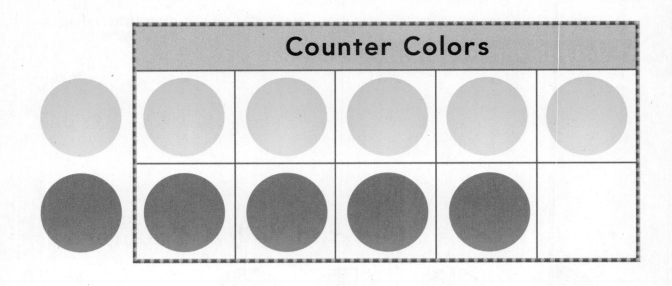

Counter Colors

DIRECTIONS 1. Billy made a graph showing his counters. Color the counters to show his categories. How many counters are in each category? Write the numbers. 2. Circle the category that has more counters on the graph.

Share and Show

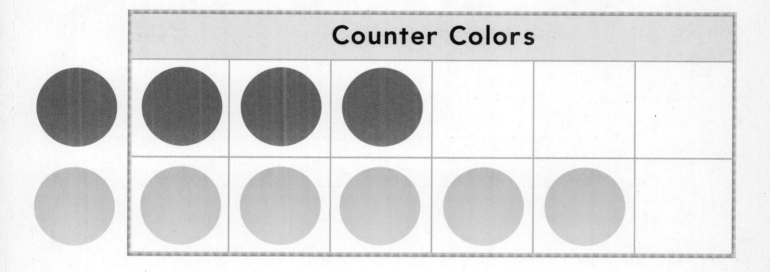

Counter Colors

 3 ◉

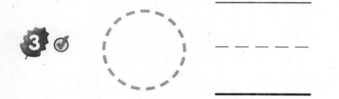   

4 ❀

DIRECTIONS 3. Rong made a graph of her counters. Color the counters to show
her categories. How many counters are in each category? Write the numbers.
4. Circle the category that has fewer counters on the graph.

On Your Own Real World

WRITE Math

5

Cube Colors				

_ _ _ _ _

_ _ _ _ _

DIRECTIONS 5. Brian has more blue cubes than red cubes. Draw and color to show his cubes on the graph. Count how many in each category. Write the numbers.

HOME ACTIVITY • Have your child tell about the graph he or she made on this page. Ask him or her which category has more cubes and which category has fewer cubes.

Read a Graph

Common
Core

COMMON CORE STANDARD—K.MD.B.3
*Classify objects and count the number of objects
in each category.*

Counter Colors

R	R	R	R	R	
Y	Y	Y	Y		

 1.

2.

R   Y

DIRECTIONS 1. Color the counters to show the categories.
R is for red, and Y is for yellow. How many counters are in each
category? Write the numbers. **2.** Circle the category that has
more counters on the graph.

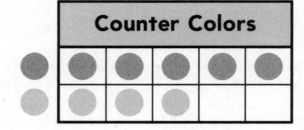

Counter Colors

_____   _____

○   ○   - - - - - -   - - - - - -

_____   _____

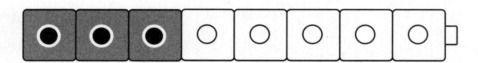

_____   _____

8 = = =   - - - - -   + - -   - - - -

_____   _____

DIRECTIONS 1. How many counters are in each category? Write the numbers. Circle the category that has more counters. **2.** Complete the addition sentence to show the numbers that match the cube train. **3.** Make a cube train that is about the same length as the cube train shown. Draw and color the cube train.

FOR MORE PRACTICE
GO TO THE
Personal Math Trainer

Chapter 12 Review/Test

 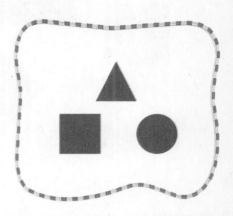

  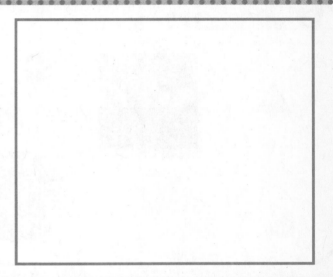

  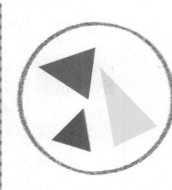  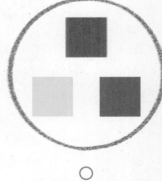

○   ○   ○

DIRECTIONS 1. Lin sorted some shapes into categories by color. Look at the shape at the beginning of the row. Mark an X on the category that shows where the shape belongs. **2.** Draw and color a shape that belongs in this category. **3.** Look at the shape at the beginning of the row. Mark under all of the categories the shape can belong.

GO DIGITAL Assessment Options **Chapter Test**

4

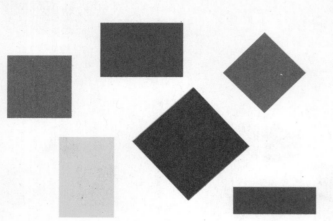

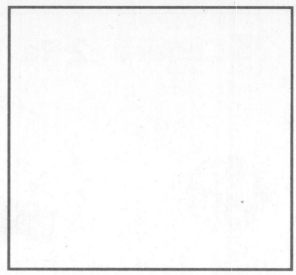

Personal Math Trainer

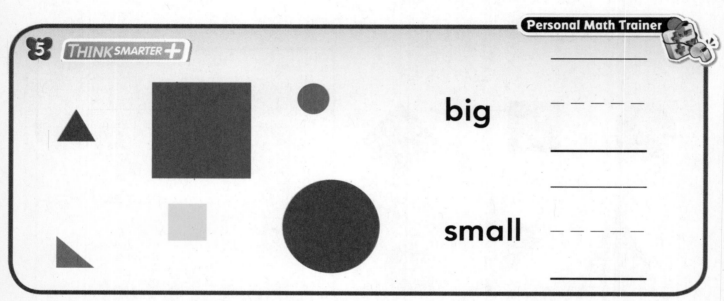

big

small

_____

- - - - - - -

_____

_____

- - - - - - -

_____

6

Big	Small

Big	Small

○   ○

DIRECTIONS 4. Draw and color a shape that belongs in this category.
5. Mark an X on each big shape. Write how many big objects. Draw a circle around each of the small objects. Write how many small objects. **6.** Mark under the chart that shows the shapes correctly classified.

718 seven hundred eighteen

7 THINK SMARTER +

Triangles and Circles

_____   _____

- - - - - - -   - - - - - - -

● _____   ▲ _____

8

Blue Squares and Circles

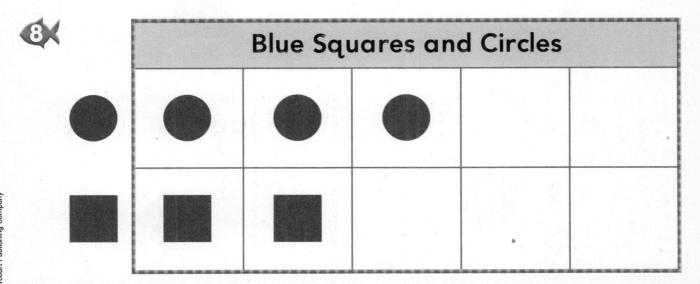

DIRECTIONS 7. Sort and classify the shapes by category. Draw each shape on the graph. Write how many of each shape. 8. Jake sorted some shapes. Then he made a graph. Count how many shapes there are in each category. Mark an X on the category that has more shapes.

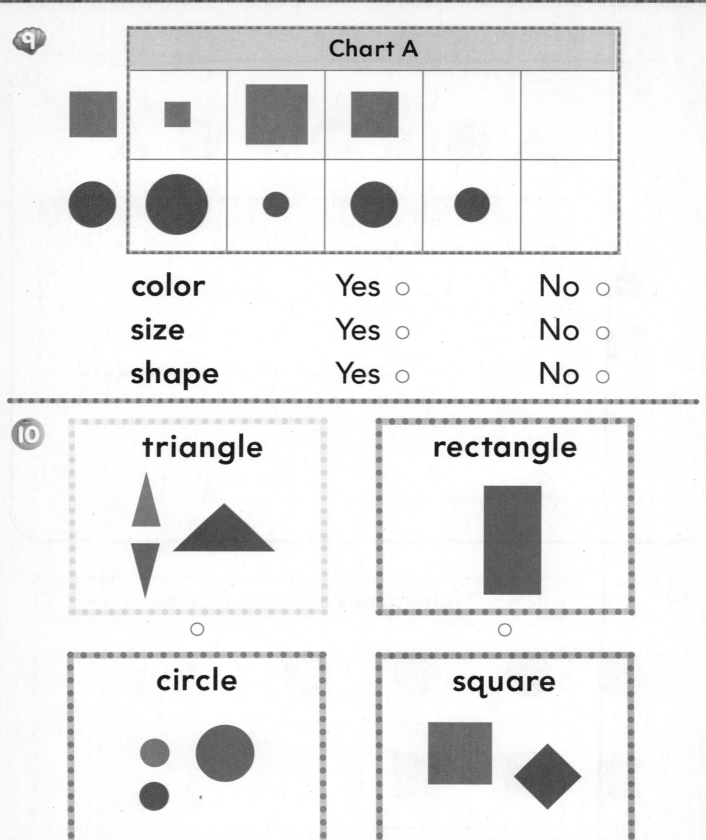

9

Chart A				

color   Yes ○   No ○

size   Yes ○   No ○

shape   Yes ○   No ○

10

triangle

rectangle
○

○

circle

square
○

○

DIRECTIONS **9.** Is this chart sorted by color, size, and shape? Choose
Yes or No. **10.** Choose all of the sets with the same number of objects.

720 seven hundred twenty

Picture Glossary

above [arriba, encima]

The kite is **above** the rabbit.

add [sumar]

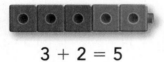

$$3 + 2 = 5$$

alike [igual]

and [y]

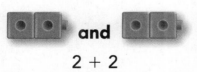

$$2 + 2$$

behind [detrás]

The box is **behind** the girl.

below [debajo]

The rabbit is **below** the kite.

beside [al lado]

The tree is **beside** the bush.

big [grande]

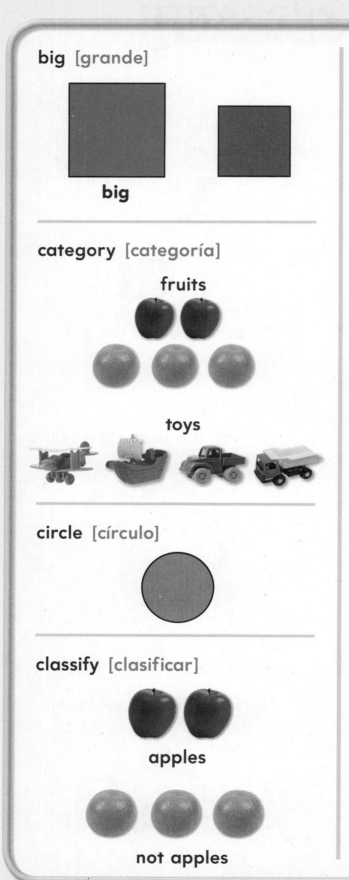

big

category [categoría]

fruits

toys

circle [círculo]

classify [clasificar]

apples

not apples

color [color]

red
[rojo]

blue
[azul]

yellow
[amarillo]

green
[verde]

orange
[anaranjado]

compare [comparar]

cone [cono]

corner [esquina]

corner

cube [cubo]

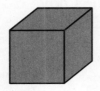

curve [curva]

curved surface
[superficie curva]

Some solids have
a **curved surface.**

cylinder [cilindro]

different [diferente]

eight [ocho]

eighteen [dieciocho]

eleven [once]

fewer [menos]

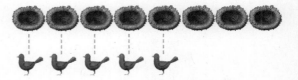

3 **fewer** birds

fifteen [quince]

fifty [cincuenta]

1	2	3	4	5	6	7	8	9	10
11	12	13	14	15	16	17	18	19	20
21	22	23	24	25	26	27	28	29	30
31	32	33	34	35	36	37	38	39	40
41	42	43	44	45	46	47	48	49	50

five [cinco]

flat [plano]

A circle is a **flat** shape.

flat surface [superficie plana]

Some solids have a flat **surface**.

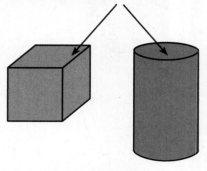

four [cuatro]

fourteen [catorce]

graph [gráfica]

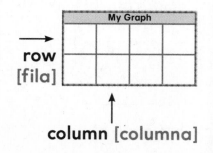

row [fila]

column [columna]

greater [mayor]

9 is greater than 6

6

9

---

heavier [más pesado]

↑

heavier

---

hexagon [hexágono]

---

in front of [delante de]

The box is **in front of** the girl.

---

is equal to [es igual a]

3 + 2 = 5

3 + 2 **is equal to** 5

---

larger [más grande]

2   3

A quantity of 3 is **larger** than a quantity of 2.

---

less [menor/menos]

9 is **less** than 11

9

11

---

lighter [más liviano]

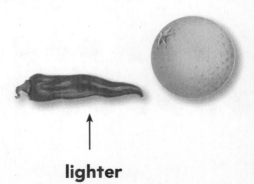

↑

lighter

longer [más largo]

 **longer**

---

match [emparejar]

---

minus – [menos]

$4 - 3 = 1$

4 **minus** 3 is equal to 1

---

more [más]

2 **more** leaves

next to [al lado de]

The bush is **next to** the tree.

---

nine [nueve]

---

nineteen [diecinueve]

---

one [uno]

one hundred [cien]

1	2	3	4	5	6	7	8	9	10
11	12	13	14	15	16	17	18	19	20
21	22	23	24	25	26	27	28	29	30
31	32	33	34	35	36	37	38	39	40
41	42	43	44	45	46	47	48	49	50
51	52	53	54	55	56	57	58	59	60
61	62	63	64	65	66	67	68	69	70
71	72	73	74	75	76	77	78	79	80
81	82	83	84	85	86	87	88	89	90
91	92	93	94	95	96	97	98	99	100

ones [unidades]

3 **ones**

pairs [pares]

3

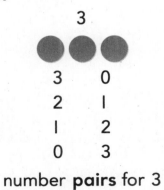

3	0
2	1
1	2
0	3

number **pairs** for 3

plus + [más]

2 **plus** 1 is equal to 3

$2 + 1 = 3$

rectangle [rectángulo]

roll [rodar]

same height
[de la misma altura]

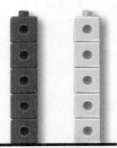

same length [del mismo largo]

same number
[el mismo número]

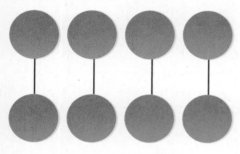

same weight [del mismo peso]

seven [siete]

seventeen [diecisiete]

shape [forma]

shorter [más corto]

shorter

side [lado]

side

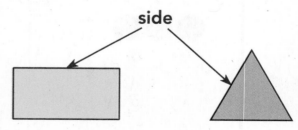

sides of equal length [lados del mismo largo]

six [seis]

sixteen [dieciséis]

size [tamaño]

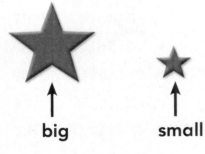

big   small

slide [deslizar]

small [pequeño]

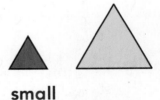

small

solid [sólido]

solid

A cylinder is a **solid** shape.

sphere [esfera]

square [cuadrado]

stack [apilar]

subtract [restar]

Subtract to find out how many are left.

taller [más alto]

taller

ten [diez]

tens [decenas]

1	2	3	4	5	6	7	8	9	10
11	12	13	14	15	16	17	18	19	20
21	22	23	24	25	26	27	28	29	30
31	32	33	34	35	36	37	38	39	40
41	42	43	44	45	46	47	48	49	50
51	52	53	54	55	56	57	58	59	60
61	62	63	64	65	66	67	68	69	70
71	72	73	74	75	76	77	78	79	80
81	82	83	84	85	86	87	88	89	90
91	92	93	94	95	96	97	98	99	100

tens

thirteen [trece]

three [tres]

three-dimensional shapes
[figuras tridimensionales]

triangle [triángulo]

twelve [doce]

twenty [veinte]

two [dos]

two-dimensional shapes
[figuras bidimensionales]

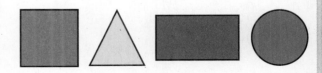

vertex [vértice]

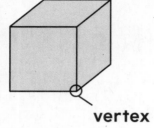

vertex

---

vertices [vértices]

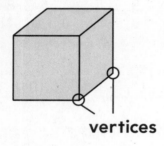

vertices

---

zero, none [cero, ninguno]

zero fish

Correlations

© Houghton Mifflin Harcourt Publishing Company

 COMMON CORE STATE STANDARDS

Standards You Will Learn

Mathematical Practices		Some examples are:
MP1	Make sense of problems and persevere in solving them.	Lessons 1.3, 1.5, 1.9, 3.9, 5.1, 5.3, 5.4, 5.6, 5.7, 6.1, 6.3, 6.4, 6.5, 6.6, 7.6, 11.3, 11.5
MP2	Reason abstractly and quantitatively.	Lessons 1.1, 1.2, 1.3, 1.4, 1.5, 1.6, 1.8, 1.9, 1.10, 2.2, 2.3, 2.5, 3.2, 3.4, 3.6, 3.8, 4.2, 4.4, 5.1, 5.2, 5.3, 5.4, 5.5, 5.6, 5.7, 5.8, 5.9, 5.10, 5.11, 5.12, 6.1, 6.2, 6.3, 6.4, 6.5, 6.6, 6.7, 7.1, 7.2, 7.3, 7.4, 7.5, 7.6, 7.7, 7.8, 7.9, 7.10, 8.1, 8.2, 8.3, 9.4, 9.6, 9.8, 9.10, 10.3, 10.4, 10.5, 12.1, 12.2, 12.3, 12.4, 12.5
MP3	Construct viable arguments and critique the reasoning of others.	Lessons 2.1, 2.2, 2.3, 2.4, 2.5, 3.9, 7.1, 7.3, 7.7, 7.9, 10.7, 10.9, 10.10, 11.1, 11.2, 11.3, 11.4, 11.5
MP4	Model with mathematics.	Lessons 1.7, 1.9, 2.4, 3.1, 3.9, 4.1, 4.3, 4.5, 5.2, 5.3, 5.4, 6.2, 6.3, 6.4, 7.6, 8.4, 10.6, 10.8, 10.9, 10.10
MP5	Use appropriate tools strategically.	Lessons 1.8, 2.1, 2.2, 2.3, 2.4, 3.1, 3.3, 3.5, 3.7, 4.1, 4.5, 5.2, 6.2, 6.7, 7.5, 8.1, 8.4, 9.1, 9.2, 9.3, 9.5, 9.7, 9.9, 9.11, 9.12, 10.1, 10.2, 10.3, 10.4, 10.5, 10.6, 11.1, 11.2, 11.4, 12.1, 12.2, 12.3
MP6	Attend to precision.	Lessons 2.5, 4.6, 4.7, 8.1, 8.7, 9.1, 9.3, 9.5, 9.7, 9.9, 10.1, 10.2, 10.3, 10.4, 10.5, 10.9, 10.10, 11.1, 11.2, 11.3, 11.4, 11.5, 12.1, 12.2, 12.3, 12.4, 12.5
MP7	Look for and make use of structure.	Lessons 1.7, 1.8, 3.1, 3.3, 3.5, 3.7, 4.3, 5.5, 5.8, 5.9, 5.10, 5.11, 5.12, 7.1, 7.2, 7.3, 7.4, 7.5, 7.7, 7.8, 7.9, 7.10, 8.5, 8.6, 8.7, 8.8, 9.1, 9.2, 9.3, 9.4, 9.5, 9.6, 9.7, 9.8, 9.9, 9.10, 9.11, 9.12, 10.1, 10.2, 10.6

Standards You Will Learn

Mathematical Practices		Some examples are:
MP8	Look for and express regularity in repeated reasoning.	Lessons 3.3, 3.5, 3.7, 4.5, 4.6, 4.7, 5.5, 6.7, 7.2, 7.4, 7.8, 7.10, 8.5, 8.6, 8.7, 8.8, 9.4, 9.6, 9.8, 9.10, 9.11, 9.12, 10.7, 12.4, 12.5
Domain: Counting and Cardinality		**Student Edition Lessons**
Know number names and the count sequence.		
K.CC.A.1	Count to 100 by ones and by tens.	Lessons 8.5, 8.6, 8.7, 8.8
K.CC.A.2	Count forward beginning from a given number within the known sequence (instead of having to begin at 1).	Lessons 4.4, 8.3, 8.5
K.CC.A.3	Write numbers from 0 to 20. Represent a number of objects with a written numeral 0–20 (with 0 representing a count of no objects).	Lessons 1.2, 1.4, 1.6, 1.9, 1.10, 3.2, 3.4, 3.6, 3.8, 4.2, 8.2
Count to tell the number of objects.		
K.CC.B.4a	Understand the relationship between numbers and quantities; connect counting to cardinality. a. When counting objects, say the number names in the standard order, pairing each object with one and only one number name and each number name with one and only one object.	Lessons 1.1, 1.3, 1.5
K.CC.B.4b	Understand the relationship between numbers and quantities; connect counting to cardinality. b. Understand that the last number name said tells the number of objects counted. The number of objects is the same regardless of their arrangement or the order in which they were counted.	Lesson 1.7
K.CC.B.4c	Understand the relationship between numbers and quantities; connect counting to cardinality. c. Understand that each successive number name refers to a quantity that is one larger.	Lesson 1.8

Domain: Counting and Cardinality		
Count to tell the number of objects.		
K.CC.B.5	Count to answer "how many?" questions about as many as 20 things arranged in a line, a rectangular array, or a circle, or as many as 10 things in a scattered configuration; given a number from 1–20, count out that many objects.	Lessons 3.1, 3.3, 3.5, 3.7, 4.1, 8.1
Compare numbers.		
K.CC.C.6	Identify whether the number of objects in one group is greater than, less than, or equal to the number of objects in another group, e.g., by using matching and counting strategies.	Lessons 2.1, 2.2, 2.3, 2.4, 2.5, 3.9, 4.5, 4.6, 8.4
K.CC.C.7	Compare two numbers between 1 and 10 presented as written numerals.	Lessons 3.9, 4.7, 8.6
Domain: Operations and Algebraic Thinking		
Understand addition as putting together and adding to, and understand subtraction as taking apart and taking from.		
K.OA.A.1	Represent addition and subtraction with objects, fingers, mental images, drawings, sounds (e.g., claps), acting out situations, verbal explanations, expressions, or equations.	Lessons 5.1, 5.2, 5.3, 6.1, 6.2, 6.3
K.OA.A.2	Solve addition and subtraction word problems, and add and subtract within 10, e.g., by using objects or drawings to represent the problem.	Lessons 5.7, 6.6, 6.7
K.OA.A.3	Decompose numbers less than or equal to 10 into pairs in more than one way, e.g., by using objects or drawings, and record each decomposition by a drawing or equation (e.g., $5 = 2 + 3$ and $5 = 4 + 1$).	Lessons 1.7, 4.1, 5.8, 5.9, 5.10, 5.11, 5.12

Standards You Will Learn

Domain: Operations and Algebraic Thinking		
Understand addition as putting together and adding to, and understand subtraction as taking apart and taking from.		
K.OA.A.4	For any number from 1 to 9, find the number that makes 10 when added to the given number, e.g., by using objects or drawings, and record the answer with a drawing or equation.	Lessons 4.3, 5.5
K.OA.A.5	Fluently add and subtract within 5.	Lessons 5.4, 5.6, 6.4, 6.5
Domain: Number and Operations in Base Ten		
Work with numbers 11–19 to gain foundations for place value.		
K.NBT.A.1	Compose and decompose numbers from 11 to 19 into ten ones and some further ones, e.g., by using objects or drawings, and record each composition or decomposition by a drawing or equation (e.g., 18 = 10 + 8); understand that these numbers are composed of ten ones and one, two, three, four, five, six, seven, eight, or nine ones.	Lessons 7.1, 7.2, 7.3, 7.4, 7.5, 7.7, 7.8, 7.9, 7.10
Domain: Measurement and Data		
Describe and compare measurable attributes.		
K.MD.A.1	Describe measurable attributes of objects, such as length or weight. Describe several measurable attributes of a single object.	Lesson 11.5
K.MD.A.2	Directly compare two objects with a measurable attribute in common, to see which object has "more of"/ "less of" the attribute, and describe the difference.	Lessons 11.1, 11.2, 11.3, 11.4

Common Core State Standards © Copyright 2010. National Governors Association Center for Best Practices and Council of Chief State School Officers. All rights reserved. This product is not sponsored or endorsed by the Common Core State Standards Initiative of the National Governors Association Center for Best Practices and the Council of Chief State School Officers.

Domain: Measurement and Data		
Classify objects and count the number of objects in each category.		
K.MD.B.3	Classify objects into given categories; count the numbers of objects in each category and sort the categories by count.	Lessons 12.1, 12.2, 12.3, 12.4, 12.5
Domain: Geometry		
Identify and describe shapes (squares, circles, triangles, rectangles, hexagons, cubes, cones, cylinders, and spheres).		
K.G.A.1	Describe objects in the environment using names of shapes, and describe the relative positions of these objects using terms such as *above, below, beside, in front of, behind,* and *next to.*	Lessons 10.8, 10.9, 10.10
K.G.A.2	Correctly name shapes regardless of their orientations or overall size.	Lessons 9.1, 9.3, 9.5, 9.7, 9.9, 10.2, 10.3, 10.4, 10.5
K.G.A.3	Identify shapes as two-dimensional (lying in a plane, "flat") or three-dimensional ("solid").	Lesson 10.6
Analyze, compare, create, and compose shapes.		
K.G.B.4	Analyze and compare two- and three-dimensional shapes, in different sizes and orientations, using informal language to describe their similarities, differences, parts (e.g., number of sides and vertices / "corners") and other attributes (e.g., having sides of equal length).	Lessons 9.2, 9.4, 9.6, 9.8, 9.10, 9.11, 10.1
K.G.B.5	Model shapes in the world by building shapes from components (e.g., sticks and clay balls) and drawing shapes.	Lesson 10.7
K.G.B.6	Compose simple shapes to form larger shapes.	Lesson 9.12

Index

Eighteen
count, 409–412, 415–418
model, 409–412
write, 415–418

Eleven
count, 361–364, 367–370
model, 361–364
write, 367–370

Equations
addition, 243–246, 249–251, 255–258,
261–264, 267–270, 273, 276,
279–282, 285–288, 291–294,
297–300
subtraction, 323–326, 329–331,
335–338, 341–344

Essential Question. In every Student
Edition lesson. Some examples are: 13,
43, 311, 329, 687, 705

Expressions
addition, 231–234, 237–240
subtraction, 311–314, 317–320

Family Involvement
Family Note. *See* Family Note
Home Activity. *See* Home Activity

Fifteen
count, 385–388
draw a picture, 391–393
model, 385–388
use numbers to, 391–393
write, 385–388

Fifty, 453–456

Five
compare
numbers to, 81–84, 87–90, 93–95,
99–102, 105–108
by counting sets to, 105–108
by matching sets to, 99–102
count, 37–40, 43–46
draw, 37–40, 46
fluently add within, 231–234,
243–246, 249–251, 273–276
fluently subtract within, 311–314,
323–326, 329–331, 335–338
model, 37–40

ways to make, 49–52
write, 43–46

Five frames, 13–15, 25–27, 37–39, 81–82,
87–88, 93–94

Flat, 603–606, 609–612. *See also*
Two-Dimensional Shapes.

Flat surface, 586, 592, 598

Four
count, 25–28, 31–33
draw, 25–28
model, 25–28
write, 31–33

Fourteen
count, 373–376, 379–382
model, 373–376
write, 379–382

G

Games
At the Farm, 686
Bus Stop, 12
Connecting Cube Challenge, 648
Counting to Blastoff, 80
Follow the Shapes, 572
Number Line Up, 118
Number Picture, 492
Pairs That Make 7, 230
Spin and Count!, 180
Spin for More, 310
Sweet and Sour Path, 360
Who Has More?, 428

Geometry, 481–488 *See* Shapes;
Three-dimensional shapes;
Two-dimensional shapes

Glossary, H1–H12

Graph, concrete, 705–708, 711–714

Greater, 87–90

Guided Practice. *See* Share and Show

H

Hands On, 13–19, 25–28, 37–40, 49–52,
55–58, 81–84, 87–90, 93–95, 119–122,
131–134, 143–146, 155–158, 181–184,

193–196, 237–240, 249–251, 273–276, 279–282, 285–288, 291–294, 297–300, 317–320, 329–331, 347–350, 361–364, 373–376, 385–388, 397–400, 409–412, 429–432, 553–556, 573–576, 579–582, 585–588, 591–594, 597–599, 609–612, 649–652, 655–658, 667–670, 687–690, 693–696, 699–701, 705–708

Heavier, 667–670

Heights
    compare, 655–658, 673–676

Hexagon
    identify and name, 541–544
    describe, 547–550
    sides, 547–550
    vertices, 547–550

Home Activity, 16, 22, 28, 33, 40, 46, 52, 58, 64, 70, 84, 90, 95, 102, 108, 122, 128, 134, 139, 146, 152, 158, 164, 170, 184, 190, 196, 201, 208, 214, 220, 234, 240, 246, 258, 264, 270, 276, 282, 288, 294, 300, 314, 320, 326, 331, 338, 344, 350, 364, 370, 376, 382, 388, 393, 400, 406, 412, 418, 432, 438, 444, 449, 456, 462, 468, 474, 496, 502, 508, 514, 520, 525, 532, 538, 544, 550, 556, 562, 576, 582, 588, 594, 599, 606, 612, 618, 624, 630, 652, 658, 663, 670, 676, 690, 696, 701, 708, 714

Hundred
    count by ones to, 459–462
    count by tens to, 465–468

Hundred chart, 459–462, 465–468

In front of, 627–630
Is equal to, 243–248

Larger, 55–58
Lengths
    compare, 649–652, 673–676
Less, 93–95

Lighter, 667–670
Listen and Draw
    activity, 25, 87, 93, 131, 143, 155, 193, 199, 237, 249, 255, 273, 279, 285, 291, 297, 317, 329, 347, 361, 367, 373, 379, 385, 397, 403, 409, 415, 429, 435, 441, 453, 459, 465, 511, 523, 535, 547, 553, 573, 655, 687, 693, 699, 705
    Real World, 13, 19, 31, 37, 43, 49, 55, 67, 81, 105, 119, 125, 137, 149, 161, 181, 187, 211, 217, 231, 261, 267, 311, 335, 341, 471, 493, 499, 505, 517, 529, 541, 579, 585, 591, 597, 609, 615, 621, 627, 649, 655, 667, 673

Longer, 649–652

Manipulatives and Materials
    bead string, 364, 376, 388, 400, 412, 421, 432
    cone, 597–600
    connecting cubes, 310
    counters, two–color, 50–52, 121, 133, 145, 157
    Number and Symbol Tiles, 347
    three-dimensional shapes, 573–576, 603–606, 609–612
    two-dimensional shapes, 553–556, 603–606, 609–612

Matching
    compare by, 99–102, 205–208

Mathematical Practices. In many lessons. Some examples are:
1. Make sense of problems and persevere in solving them. In many lessons. Some examples are: 25, 37, 61, 167, 231, 243, 249, 261, 267, 311, 323, 329, 335, 341, 391, 673
2. Reason abstractly and quantitatively. In many lessons. Some examples are: 13, 19, 25, 31, 37, 43, 55, 61, 67, 87, 231, 237, 243, 249, 255, 261, 267, 273, 279, 285, 511, 523, 535, 547, 585, 591, 597, 687, 693, 699, 705

3. Construct viable arguments and critique the reasoning of others. In many lessons. Some examples are: 81, 87, 93, 99, 105, 167, 361, 373, 397, 409, 447, 609, 621, 627, 649, 655, 661, 667, 673

4. Model with mathematics. In many lessons. Some examples are: 49, 61, 99, 119, 167, 181, 193, 205, 237, 243, 249, 317, 323, 329, 391, 447, 541, 603, 615, 621, 627

5. Use appropriate tools strategically. In many lessons. Some examples are: 55, 81, 87, 93, 99, 119, 131, 143, 155, 181, 205, 237, 317, 347, 385, 429, 447, 493, 499, 505, 517, 529, 541, 553, 559, 573, 579, 585, 591, 597

6. Attend to precision. In many lessons. Some examples are: 105, 211, 217, 429, 465, 493, 499, 505, 517, 529, 573, 579, 585, 591, 597, 621, 627, 649, 655, 661, 667, 673, 687, 693, 699, 705, 711

7. Look for and make use of structure. In many lessons. Some examples are: 49, 55, 119, 131, 143, 155, 193, 255, 273, 279, 285, 291, 297, 361, 367, 373, 379, 385, 397, 511, 517, 523, 529, 535, 541, 547, 553, 559, 573, 579, 603

8. Look for and express regularity in repeated reasoning. In many lessons. Some examples are: 131, 143, 155, 205, 211, 217, 255, 347, 367, 379, 403, 415, 453, 459, 465, 471, 511, 523, 535, 547, 553, 559, 609, 705, 711

ten, 181–184, 187–190, 199–201,
    205–208, 211–214, 297–300
three, 25–28, 31–33
twelve, 361–364, 367–370
twenty, 429–432, 435–438, 441–444
two, 13–16, 19–22
use to 15, 391–393
ways to make 5, 49–52
ways to make 10, 193–196
write, 19–22, 31–33, 43–46, 67–70,
    125–128, 137–139, 149–152,
    161–164, 187–190, 367–370,
    379–382, 385–388, 403–406,
    415–418, 435–438
zero, 61–64, 67–70

One/Ones
    count, 13–16, 19–22, 361–364
    draw, 13–16, 22
    model, 13–16, 361–364
    write, 19–22

On Your Own. *See* Problem Solving

Order
    numbers
        to five, 55–58
        to ten, 199–202
        to twenty, 441–444

Pair, 49–52

Personal Math Trainer. In all Student
    Edition lessons. Some examples are:
    10, 75, 76, 78, 113, 114, 116, 175, 176,
    178, 225, 226, 228, 304, 305, 308, 353,
    356, 358, 422, 423, 426, 479, 480, 490,
    566, 568, 570, 633, 634, 646, 680, 681,
    684, 718, 719

Picture Glossary. *See* Glossary

Plus, 237–240, 243–246, 249–251,
    255–258, 261–264, 267–270, 273–276,
    279–282, 285–288, 297–300

Position words
    above, 615–618
    behind, 627–630
    below, 615–618
    beside, 621–624
    in front of, 627–630
    next to, 621–624

Practice and Homework. In every
    Student Edition lesson. Some
    examples are: 185–186, 247–248,
    321–322, 445–446, 515–516, 601–602,
    671–672

Problem Solving
    activity, 22, 46, 52, 58, 184, 190, 196,
        270, 344, 350, 462, 468, 496, 502,
        508, 514, 520, 532, 538, 556, 576,
        690, 696, 708
    On Your Own, 64, 170, 208, 562, 606
    Real World activity, 16, 28, 40, 70, 84,
        90, 108, 122, 128, 134, 146, 152,
        158, 164, 214, 220, 234, 240, 258,
        264, 276, 282, 288, 294, 300, 314,
        320, 338, 364, 370, 376, 382, 388,
        400, 406, 412, 418, 432, 438, 444,
        456, 474, 544, 550, 582, 588, 594,
        612, 618, 624, 630, 652, 658, 670,
        676, 714
    Real World On Your Own, 102, 246,
        326
    Real World Unlock the Problem, 61,
        99, 167, 243, 323, 391, 603, 661
    strategies
        act out addition problems, 243–245
        act out subtraction problems,
            323–325
        draw a picture, 167–170, 391–393,
            559–562, 661–663
        make a model, 61–64, 99–102,
            205–208, 447–449
    Unlock the Problem, 205, 447, 559

Put Together, 237–240, 249–251, 255–258

Reading
    numbers. *See* Numbers